tried & true

all season grilling & bbq

top 200 recipes

printing specifications

This book was produced from an Adobe® Acrobat® PDF file using the following digital production equipment:

- Xerox® FreeFlow™ front end
- The Xerox® DP525/1050 duplex printing system.
- Parallel Turnbar configuration featuring the maximum flexibility Multiplex 3 engine system
- Xerox® Print Line Bus technology.
- Text printed on Enterprise 60 lb. Digital Opaque "Plus" Satin "92" Brightness
- Cover printed on Xerox® iGen3® Digital Press using Xerox® Digital Color Xpressions 100 lb. Cover

Pre/post system comprised of:
- Lasermax Roll Systems Unwinder
- WEKO web conditioning
- Lasermax Roll Systems Cutter
- MBO Signature Folder
- Palamides Alpha 500 Signature Stacker
- Shuttleworth Transport
- Müller-Martini Sigma Binding Line with 3 knife trimming

We would like to thank the Enterprise Group, a Weyerhaeuser Company, for the Continuous Feed paper they supplied for this show.

Special thanks to Allrecipes.com for granting permission to produce this promotional copy of the *Tried & True - All Season Grilling & BBQ* cookbook.

all season grilling & bbq

top 200 recipes

Published by Allrecipes.com, Inc.
400 Mercer Street, Suite 302, Seattle, WA 98109

Allrecipes, Allrecipes.com, and Cookierecipe.com are trademarks or registered trademarks of Allrecipes.com, Inc.

For distribution information, contact Allrecipes.

Printed and bound in Canada.
Second Edition March 2005

Library of Congress Cataloging-in-Publication data is on file with the publisher.

10 9 8 7 6 5 4 3 2 1

ISBN 0-9711-7236-6

EDITOR: Syd Carter
FOOD EDITOR: Jennifer Anderson
PRODUCTION MANAGER: Jill Charing
RECIPE EDITORS: Emily Brune, Richard Kozel, Lesley Peterson
CREATIVE DIRECTOR: Yann Oehl
ART DIRECTOR: Jeff Cummings

Cover photograph: ©StockFood/Comet

dedication

This book is dedicated to those devoted to the smoke, the spice, and the flavors of the grill, no matter what the weather.

acknowledgments

* *

The book you are holding is a community cookbook: the recipes within come from the community of cooks who gather online at Allrecipes.com. It is the members of this community, first and foremost, who we would like to thank - anyone that has shared, reviewed, requested, or tried an Allrecipes recipe. The success of the Allrecipes community resides in your experience, enthusiasm, and generosity.

In addition, a huge debt of thanks is owed to the staff of Allrecipes - the people who have dedicated themselves to building a helpful, supportive environment for our community.

table of contents

introduction

There's an excitement surrounding a meal from the grill that just doesn't compare to any other cooking method. The stove is a means to an end, whereas the grill is the main event. Not just a cooking method, grilling is an activity, the centerpiece of a party or dinner, a way of life, a lifestyle statement, a symbol of leisure, relaxation and happiness, all while engaging in the oldest cooking method known to the human race. And then there's the simple fact that pretty much everything tastes better on the grill. The fun you have in cooking it, the smoke, and the mouthwatering caramelization and browning of foods that high heat always ensures - all these factors together create a taste that cannot be beat.

Grilling is no longer just for summer, either. More and more people have taken on outdoor grilling as a year-round pursuit, thinking that holding an umbrella in one hand and tongs in the other is a small price to pay for righteous ribs in January. If you're not so lucky as to have a covered patio or an iron constitution, electric countertop models will serve you until the weather clears. Most of these recipes in this book will work well on those, as well as under the broiler or in a cast iron pan.

We here at Allrecipes.com have selected some of our all-time highest rated barbeque recipes for this book. Every recipe has won repeated standing ovations from the people who have tried it, creative cooks, and picky eaters alike. Even better than a traditional cookbook (where the recipes are tested once or twice), each of the recipes you'll find on the following pages has been tested many times - not by culinary professionals in specially equipped test kitchens, but in the home kitchens of people like you.

In this book, we also provide some simple tips for getting the most out of your grill. Suggestions for helpful tools, organizing tips for outdoor cooking, and flavor enhancing techniques can all be found out in Cooking Basics chapter. Grilling charts with approximate grilling times for specific types and cuts of meat are on pages 23 - 25. Looking for a quick and easy recipe that you can serve your family tonight? Many recipes in this book, although simple to prepare, do take some time - but most of that time is used for marinating the food. The time you actually spend preparing the food and cooking it is minimal. However when time is short, recipes that take less than an hour can be found in the index on page 282 under the heading "quick and easy."

what's the difference?

Unless you come from a family of fiercely dedicated barbeque masters, chances are you grew up using the terms "grilling" and "barbequing" interchangeably. As cooking with fire becomes a year-round passion in more homes, though, more people are learning the difference, and yes indeed, there is a difference. Though the subtle nuances of both arts could inspire entire books by themselves, the real distinction comes down to a basic question of heat: how hot is it, and where is it coming from?

Grilling is what happens when you put food directly over fire, to be cooked quickly, usually at a high temperature (between 350 and 550 degrees F). Grilling works best for smaller pieces of food that are naturally tender. With barbequing, you cook meat with smoke and indirect heat-that is, the fire is near the food but not directly under it--for longer periods of time, at lower temperatures (between 200 and 300 degrees F). Barbequing is the method to use for large pieces of meat that take long, slow cooking to become tender and succulent.

The gas versus charcoal debate has been going on for a long time. Charcoal grills are cheaper to buy and cheaper to fuel. Gas is more convenient though-just turn it on, preheat for a short time, and you're good to go, with no coals to stack and wait for. Gas offers greater heat control, and most gas grills come with a temperature gauge. However, charcoal proponents argue that there's no beating the smoky flavor created by those coals.

cooking basics

On the following pages you will find tips for grilling. Hone your skills with our handy step-by-step instructions for everything from setting up your grill to tips for making use of marinades and rubs to advice for cooking the perfect burger. We have even included our grilling time charts for different cuts of meat and poultry.

getting started

Everything tastes better on the grill, and nothing could be simpler, right? Well...
there is more to barbeque than tossing a steak on the grill. Experience is a great teacher,
but before you spend years perfecting that secret recipe, you might want to go over
the basics.

preheating the grill

Whether you are using a new gas grill, the standard kettle charcoal grill, a grill pan, or
your oven's broiler, you will need to preheat. Before you start, read the recipe. Are you
cooking over direct heat, or indirect heat? Is the food cooked over high heat, medium
heat, or very low heat? The answers to these questions will decide how you preheat
the grill.

There are primarily two grilling methods: Cooking directly over the heat source is
known as grilling over direct heat. The food is cooked for mere minutes on a hot grill,
and the lid is rarely if ever closed. Thin cuts of meat, fillets, kabobs, satays, and vegetables are good candidates for this method. Indirect heat is used for larger pieces of meat,
such as thick steaks, roasts, and whole fish. In this method, the food is cooked just off
the heat at about 350 degrees F (175 degrees C). The lid is closed, and the cooking
times are somewhat longer. On a gas grill this generally means firing up the two outside
burners, and cooking the meat over the middle, unlit burner. When using charcoals, the
coals are pushed to the sides of the grill, leaving a place in the middle to cook.
Traditional barbeque uses a form of indirect heat using very low temperatures over long
periods of time.

the right temperature for the job

The right temperature is always important. Many gas grills come equipped with
thermometers, and reliable grill thermometers are widely available. A thermometer will
tell you exactly what heat you are working with. That being said, the standard is still the
caveman method.

This method consists of holding your hand approximately 6 inches above the coals or heat source, about the spot where the food will be cooking, and counting how many seconds you can keep your hand in this position. Count 'one-barbeque, two-barbeque...'

High Heat	3 seconds	or	500° F (260° C)
Medium High Heat	5 seconds	or	400° F (205° C)
Medium Heat	7 seconds	or	350° F (175° C)
Medium Low Heat	10 seconds	or	325° F (165° C)
Low Heat	12 seconds	or	300° F (150° C)

Once the grill is hot, scrape away any lingering debris from the grill grate with a wire brush (it's easier to remove debris when the grill is hot).

Read the instructions that come with your grill. This cannot be stressed too much. There are many, many types of grills on the market today. While some things hold true for all grills, you will find many helpful hints about everything from how to preheat the grill for the cooking method you are using to what sort of regular maintenance is required to extend the life of your grill.

useful tools

In the good old days the only tools required for cooking over an open flame were the fire and some good, long sticks. While this method is perfectly acceptable, you may wish to experiment with the innovations made during the intervening years. It seems as if everyone with a grill has a different list of necessary equipment. Over time you will discover which ones make it onto your "essentials" list, and which ones languish in a kitchen cupboard. This is our list.

· **Timer** - Useful for following those minute-by-minute instructions.

· **Skewers** - Wooden or metal skewers are essential for kabobs. Some prefer flattened skewers, which tend to inhibit the partially cooked food rolling as you turn and make it possible to cook all sides of the food. If using wooden skewers, soak in water for at least 30 minutes before threading the food onto them.

· **Disposable Drip Pans** - These are placed under food cooked using the indirect method. A drip pan catches drippings from fatty foods, preventing flare-ups. It can also be filled with water, wine, or marinade to flavor the food and provide wet heat.

- **Long Handled Tongs and Spatulas** - Used for turning foods on the grill, the long handles allow you to work from a distance.

- **Oven Mitts** - Heat resistant mitts prevent burns from working with a hot grill.

- **Basting Brushes** - Frequent basting is key to all forms of barbeque. Brushes are also useful for oiling the grate prior to placing the food on the grill.

- **Meat Thermometer** - Not strictly necessary for grilling thin cuts of meat or vegetables, a good thermometer is essential for determining the doneness of thick roasts and whole birds.

- **Fire Starter Chimney** - This is an open-topped cylindrical contraption that allows you to get your charcoal started without lighter fluid. You simply pile the coals into the chimney and insert a few paraffin starters or twists of newspaper into the holes in the bottom. When the coals are ready, dump them into the bottom of the grill and get cooking. It can be especially useful if grilling over a long period, when the fire will need refreshing regularly.

- **Grill Baskets** - These are wire baskets with long handles. A basket shaped like a fish makes turning whole fish quick and easy. Grill baskets are also used to hold small items, preventing them from falling into fire.

- **Wire Brush** - Look for one with a metal grill scraper on the front edge. This will make cleaning the grate take a matter of minutes.

- **Whisk Broom** - Handy for cleaning away ash from charcoal grills.

- **Squirt Gun** - For a little Wild West action, put out those pesky flare-ups with one of these. Also handy for anyone caught poaching off the grill.

flavor secrets

It's true that everything tastes better on the grill, but let us clue you in on all the ways you can make a good thing better, and a better thing best! A luscious marinade can define the meal, and even the most rushed barbeque chef has time to treat a piece of meat to a quick spice rub before it meets the flames. We'll also offer you the secrets of true smoky flavor, without buying any expensive equipment.

the magic behind the marinade

The idea of marinating is not a new one. For hundreds of years, cooks have been making marinades and using natural ingredients to fulfill three important functions for the meat that they cook: to flavor, to moisturize and to tenderize. The fun thing about marinades is that the formula is so flexible   you can use just about any ingredient you fancy!

The main role of marinades is to add flavor to food. A plain grilled chicken breast tastes pretty good, but a grilled chicken breast that's been bathed in an orange, ginger and sesame marinade for a few hours tastes absolutely spectacular! Start with any fresh or dried herb or spice, but don't forget about other tasty and aromatic things like fresh and dried chile peppers, onions, shallots, garlic, ginger and citrus zest.

Marinades also add moisture to foods, particularly when the marinade contains some sort of fat. Try olive, peanut, sesame, walnut or chile oil. You can also use milk, coconut milk, buttermilk, or yogurt.

Additionally, marinades are widely believed to tenderize meats. This is a controversial topic, though. It's true that the acidic ingredients in a marinade have a tenderizing effect on proteins, but since the marinade only touches the surface of the meat, not the inside, the added tenderness is usually somewhat minimal. Powdered store-bought meat tenderizers usually contain natural enzymes derived from papayas. These enzymes serve to break down the tissue of the meat, but when this kind of tenderizer is left on too long, it can make the meat mushy, so use caution.

Dairy products are the only ingredients that have been proven to tenderize meat all the way through while at the same time preserving the texture. Buttermilk and yogurt are especially popular for this purpose. Other acidic ingredients, whether or not they will significantly tenderize a piece of meat, will do a great job of balancing out the sweet, spicy and aromatic flavors of a marinade and can be just the right finishing touch you're looking for. Some of the tastiest acidic notes to add to a marinade include lemon juice and lime juice, as well as all kinds of vinegar, from cider vinegar to red or white wine vinegar, to sherry vinegar or balsamic vinegar. Also try your favorite wine, beer or liquor for a flavor that's both tangy and rich.

Wondering how long you should let the marinade work its magic? Most seafood shouldn't marinate for longer than an hour; boneless chicken breast only needs about two hours. Pork loin can soak for four hours, lamb can go from four to eight hours, and you can leave beef for 24 hours or more. More delicate meats like seafood and skinless chicken will become mushy from the acid in the marinade if they soak too long, so keep an eye on the clock.

No time to marinate? A good, flavorful alternative is a dry rub of ground spices and dried herbs. Make a big batch of your favorite rub so you'll have it on hand when the grilling urge strikes.

where there's smoke, there's flavor

It's easy to add the incomparable flavor of smoke to everything you cook. You can obtain this flavor using a smoker, using the small smoker boxes that go inside your grill, creating your own smoker box by setting an aluminum pan full of water and wood chips in the bottom of your grill, or you can simply sprinkle wood over the coals before the cooking begins. It's important to soak your wood before adding it to the fire so it will slowly give off smoke instead of just bursting into flames. Chunks should be soaked for at least an hour, chips at least 30 minutes.

There are many types of wood chips available in most stores that sell grilling gear, and each type of wood yields a slightly different flavor. Some woods complement certain meats better than others. Here's a basic guide to help you match your tastes.

- **Alder** - light, delicate flavor excellent for salmon, chicken and pork
- **Apple and Cherry** - sweet, fruity flavor that's great for poultry, game birds and pork
- **Hickory** - strong, pungent bacon-like flavor used for beef, pork and ham. This is the most popular of flavoring woods
- **Maple** - a sweet, smoky flavor ideal for game meat, poultry and pork
- **Mesquite** - a little sweeter than hickory, but still strong, this wood is great for richly flavored meats such as lamb, beef, and duck
- **Pecan** - a subtle, but rich flavor that complements any turkey or other poultry

In addition to these common woods, there are varieties of exotic woods such as plum, peach, and guava, and still other chips are made from wine and bourbon barrels.

grilling tips

You don't have to be a barbeque veteran to set yourself up for sizzling success. Get the advantage by being well set up before the flames begin. Then, find out how to select the right cuts of meat for every occasion and every budget, and make sure every last bite turns out juicy, tender, and thoroughly irresistible.

get organized

Half the trick to perfectly grilled foods is being prepared. Moving the kitchen outdoors can make for a frazzled cook, as there's always just one more thing you need from inside, and you just plain don't have the equipment and counter space you're accustomed to in your daily cooking. You'll go from harried to happy if you just take a few moments before the food hits the grill to make sure you're set up properly.

- Make sure you have plenty of fuel on hand.
- Soak wood chips and bamboo skewers if needed.
- Place you your grilling tools in easy reach.
- Prepare all ingredients before you begin grilling. Not only is it unsafe to leave a hot grill unattended, but it can be very stressful to run back and forth between your kitchen and the grill.
- In addition to the main ingredients, you will need dishes of salt and pepper for seasoning and the basting sauce you are using.
- You will need a clean plate or platter to place the meat on when it's ready. Do not place cooked meat on the board used to hold or cut raw meat.

general pointers for cooking on the grill

If you're going to be cooking delicate, low-fat foods like chicken, fish, bread, or vegetables, this is the time to oil the grill grate using a basting brush.

Do not allow raw meat and fish to come into contact with other foods. Use separate cutting boards, or thoroughly sanitize the one you are using.

When at last you lay the food on that grill, don't try to lift it up again for a couple of minutes. Initially, it will stick, and you will create a mess if you try and wrench it up again immediately. Soon enough the meat will begin to sizzle and burble and the juices and fat inside will come to the surface as they heat, causing the meat to release its iron grip on the grill grating.

Poking and stabbing the meat will cause the loss of juices that keep your meat moist and tender. Do not attempt to turn the meat with a carving fork. Instead use long handled tongs or spatulas to turn the meat. Avoid the temptation to press down on the meat with a spatula! You're not going to make it cook any faster; all you're doing is squashing out the precious juices and possibly causing flare-ups down below.

Most basting sauces can be brushed on throughout the cooking process; the exceptions are sugar-based sauces. Many commercial barbeque sauce preparations fall in this category. These tend to burn if applied too early, so apply during the last few minutes of cooking.

Any time you want to keep the fire going for more than half an hour, whether you want to cook up a second round of burgers, or you've got a brisket in there for the long haul, you'll need to add more coals to the fire before it begins to go out. Add new briquettes to the edges of the live coals as soon as the first batch is ready. By the time the first round is dying, the second round will be ready to go. Spread them out as needed, and keep on adding new coals for as long as you need the flames at the ready.

claim your steak

Choosing a steak or chop from the long row of cuts in varying sizes, shapes, and price ranges at your local market can be a positively bewildering experience. Just because something is called a "steak," does that mean it's good for grilling? Do you have to mortgage your house to afford a really good steak? Which steaks are the most tender?

Most steaks are good for grilling, although some require careful treatment in order for them to be tender enough to eat. It's possible to drop a small fortune on a prime steak, but it's certainly not necessary to spend that much for a very tender and tasty piece of beef. Some of the most tender steaks are the most expensive: the tenderloin, the porterhouse, and the T-bone. Some other steaks that are nearly as tender and just as delicious are the chuck top blade, the New York, the club, the rib-eye and the rib, the top sirloin and the round tip. If you're looking to reduce the fat in your cookout, take note that the leanest cuts of beef come from the loin and the round.

The name "London Broil" causes lots of confusion. It is actually not a specific cut of beef, but a style of cooking. The method is used with larger, cheaper cuts of meat— flank steak, top round and shoulder—to give them maximum flavor and tenderness. London broil is first marinated, and then cooked over high heat to form a dark-brown, flavorful crust on the outside. The center should be not be cooked past medium-rare, in order to maintain juiciness and flavor. Finally, the meat should be sliced very thinly, at an angle, against the grain, for the greatest possible tenderness. The ideal piece of beef for London broil weighs at least a pound, and is at least 1 inch thick.

Before you begin cooking, cut the fatty edge of steaks and chops to prevent curling. Slice through the fat at 2 to 3 inch intervals, cutting just to the meat. For perfectly grilled steaks, place them over the hottest part of the fire and leave them there for at least three minutes without moving them. When the first side is good and browned, with those picture-perfect grill lines seared into the surface, flip them and sear the other side. It's possible that, by the time the steak looks flawlessly grilled on the outside, the inside may not yet be done to your liking. In that case, simply move the steak to a cooler part of the grill to finish cooking.

build a better burger

Ah, that good ol' grilling standby, the hamburger. Everyone knows what the ideal burger should taste like—a firm, flavorful, flame-kissed exterior that gives way to the juicy, tender beefiness inside. To our great frustration, homemade burgers can often fall short of that ideal. But why?

One of the most important burger choices you can make is not in the seasoning, but in the type of ground meat you use. Our society has become more fat-conscious over the years, choosing leaner meats over fattier ones. When you make burgers with extra-lean ground meat, though, it's almost impossible to get a juicy, flavorful burger as your end result. When you're in the mood to indulge in the pure pleasure of a perfect beef hamburger, buy ground beef that is at least 15 percent fat. While you're at it, ask your butcher to freshly grind some beef just for you. You will notice a huge difference in flavor and juiciness from the prepackaged ground beef. Whether or not you're able to get custom-ground beef, keep in mind that coarsely ground meat makes a juicier burger than that which is finely ground. You can add additional moisture by mixing in a few tablespoons of tomato juice or beef broth for every pound of meat.

When mixing in flavoring and forming the meat into patties, take great pains not to over-handle the mixture or the result will be dry, unpleasantly dense burgers. There's no need to pat and squeeze your burgers into perfectly uniform discs, just press the mixture lightly until the patties stick together.

Whatever you do, DON'T mix salt into the beef, especially if you're not going to grill the patties right away. Salt will extract moisture from the meat, leaving you with bone-dry burgers. Instead, sprinkle each burger with salt right before you put it on the grill.

Besides ground beef, don't forget about ground turkey, chicken, pork, lamb, or even bulk sausage. Add ethnic flavor to your cookout by seasoning the meat with Italian, Thai, Mexican, Greek, Southwest or Middle Eastern spices. To make stuffed burgers, form a thin patty and top with a sprinkle of flavorful cheese, roasted garlic, bacon crumbles, salsa, tapenade or fresh herbs. Place another thin patty on top and carefully seal the edges. Now that's burger bliss!

the chicken challenge

To keep skinless, boneless breasts moist, tender and flavorful, flatten them to a uniform thickness so they'll cook evenly, and then marinate them. Grill them over high heat to sear the outside, and watch them carefully so they don't overcook; they should only take a few minutes per side. To cook bone-in chicken pieces perfectly, patience is key. Rub a dry spice mixture under the chicken's skin if you like, but leave the skin on to maintain moisture. Grill at a medium-low temperature, and put the lid on to keep the heat in. Turn the chicken every ten minutes or so, until there's no trace of pink left near the bones.

get your dinner in a row

Whether you call them skewers, kabobs, shish kebabs, satay, yakitori, spiedini, or brochettes, there's a specialty in just about every culture's culinary traditions involving deliciously marinated and seasoned cubes of meat threaded onto a skewer and grilled over a hot fire. When choosing meat for kebabs, buy something that's moderately tender.

If you're using bamboo skewers, soak them in water for at least 30 minutes so they won't catch on fire before their precious cargo is cooked. Make your kabobs easy to flip by threading the food onto two parallel skewers. You'll get the best results if you stick with one kind of food on each skewer since each meat and vegetable has a slightly different cooking time. It may not look quite as pretty, but your dinner will be much better when you don't have to scrape carbonized cherry tomatoes off of your perfectly cooked sirloin and your rock-hard zucchini.

grilling charts

timing is everything

The staff here at Allrecipes.com has put together some guidelines for planning your meals on the grill. Your days of sawing through an overcooked grilled steak are over (unless, of course, that's the way you like it!). We've included grilling times charts for Beef, Lamb, Ham and Fresh Pork, Chicken and Turkey.

A table of grilling times is of necessity only approximate. There are a lot of variables that can make two seemingly identical cuts of meat cook at different times - exact thickness, texture, age, and temperature of the raw meat. Until you become comfortable with cooking on the grill, the best way to determine if your meat is done is to measure the internal temperature with an instant read thermometer. Remember to insert the thermometer into the thickest part of the meat, away from the bone, for an accurate reading.

Fish requires a different doneness test. There is no temperature guideline due to the great variability between types of fish. During cooking, the fish will turn from translucent to opaque. When done, a toothpick inserted into the thickest portion should meet no resistance and come out clean when removed. Yes, the doneness test for cakes works equally well for fish!

approximate grilling times for beef

Beef should have an internal temp between 145 to 160 degrees F (63 to 70 degrees C), depending on how well done you prefer your steak and burgers.

Cut	Method	Heat	Time	Internal Temp.(min.)
Steaks - ¾ in. thick	Direct	High	3 to 5 min./side	145° F (63° C)
Steaks - 1½ in. thick	Direct	High	7 to 8 min./side	145° F (63° C)
Steaks - 2 in. thick	Direct	High	10 to 12 min./side	145° F (63° C)
Kabobs - 1 in. cubes	Direct	High	3 to 4 min./side	145° F (63° C)
Hamburger Patties - ½ in. thick	Direct	High	3 min./side	160° F (70° C)
Roast - 4 to 6 pounds	Indirect	Med	18 to 22 min./lb.	145° F (63° C)
Sirloin Tip - 3½ to 4 lbs.	Indirect	Med	20 to 25 min./lb.	145° F (63° C)
Back Ribs - single ribs	Direct	High	10 min./side	160° F (70° C)
Back Ribs - rib rack	Indirect	Med	3 hours	160° F (70° C)
Tenderloin - 2 to 3 lbs.	Direct	High	10 to 12 min./side	145° F (63° C)
Tenderloin 4 to 6 pounds	Direct	High	12 to 15 min./side	145° F (63° C)

approximate grilling times for lamb

Lamb is medium rare when the internal temperature reaches 145 degrees F (63 degrees C), and is well done at 160 degrees F (70 degrees C).

Cut	Method	Heat	Time	Internal Temp.(min.)
Chops (shoulder, loin, rib) - 1 in. thick	Direct	High	5 min./side	145° F (63° C)
Steaks (sirloin, leg) 1 in. thick	Direct	High	5 min./side	145° F (63° C)
Kabobs - 1 in. cubes	Direct	High	4 min./side	145° F (63° C)
Patties - ½ in. thick	Direct	High	3 min./side	160° F (70° C)
Leg, butterflied - 4 to 7 lbs.	Indirect	Med	40 to 50 min./total	145° F (63° C)

approximate grilling times for pork

Pork is well done at 160 degrees F (70 degrees C). Because of the risk of trichinosis, pork should be cooked to at least 144 degrees F (63 degrees C).

HAM

Cut	Method	Heat	Time	Internal Temp.(min.)
Fully Cooked - Any size	Indirect	Med	8 to 10 min./lb.	140° F (60° C)
Cook-before-eating - 10 to 14 lbs.	Indirect	Med	30 to 35 min./lb.	160° F (70° C)
Cook-before-eating - 5 to 7 lbs.	Indirect	Med	12 to 18 min./lb.	160° F (70° C)
Cook-before-eating - 3 to 4 lbs.	Indirect	Med	10 to 12 min./lb.	160° F (70° C)

FRESH PORK

Cut	Method	Heat	Time	Internal Temp.(min.)
Chops - ¾ in. thick	Direct	High	3 to 4 min./side	160° F (70° C)
Chops - 1½ in. thick	Direct	High	7 to 8 min./side	160° F (70° C)
Tenderloin - ½ to 1½ lbs.	Direct	High	7 to 12 min./side	160° F (70° C)
Ribs - 2 to 4 lbs.	Indirect	Med	1½ to 2 hours	160° F (70° C)
Patties - ½ in. thick	Direct	High	4 to 5 min./side	160° F (70° C)

approximate grilling times for chicken and poultry

Chicken and other poultry should be cooked to 180 degrees F (80 degrees C).

Cut	Method	Heat	Time	Internal Temp.(min.)
Whole Broiler or Fryer - 3 to 4 lbs.	Indirect	Med	60 to 75 min.	180° F (80° C)
Whole Roasting Hen - 5 to 7 lbs.	Indirect	Med	18 to 25 min./lb.	180° F (80° C)
Capon - 4 to 8 lbs.	Indirect	Med	15 to 20 min./lb.	180° F (80° C)
Cornish Hens - 18 to 24 oz.	Indirect	Med	45 to 55 min./side	180° F (80° C)
Breast - 6 to 8 oz.	Direct	Med/Hi	10 to 15 min./side	180° F (80° C)
Boneless Breast - 4 oz.	Direct	High	6 to 8 min./side	180° F (80° C)
Legs or Thighs - 4 to 8 oz.	Direct	Med/Hi	10 to 15 min./side	180° F (80° C)
Drumsticks - 4 oz.	Direct	Med/Hi	8 to 12 min./side	180° F (80° C)
Wings - 2 to 3 oz.	Direct	Med/Hi	8 to 12 min./side	180° F (80° C)

approximate grilling times for turkey

Turkey should be cooked to 180 degrees F (80 degrees C).

Cut	Method	Heat	Time	Internal Temp.(min.)
Fully Cooked - Any size	Indirect	Med	8 to 10 min./lb.	140° F (60° C)
Cook-before-eating - 10 to 14 lbs.	Indirect	Med	30 to 35 min./lb.	160° F (70° C)
Cook-before-eating - 5 to 7 lbs.	Indirect	Med	12 to 18 min./lb.	160° F (70° C)
Cook-before-eating - 3 to 4 lbs.	Indirect	Med	10 to 12 min./lb.	160° F (70° C)

recipe tips

variations on a theme

You may wonder why we have more than one recipe for some items, such as teriyaki marinade or burgers or Greek chicken. Don't worry--these are far from being duplicate recipes! Some dishes are so popular that our community members share multiple variations of them. In fact, when you visit Allrecipes.com, you'll find that we have dozens of variations on many of your favorite recipes. As we post new versions of a recipe, we may add a Roman numeral to the title to distinguish it (for example, the "Grilled Halibut II" recipe which appears in this book). There are lots of different ways to approach even the old standards, and in this book you can enjoy your next batch of tender, smoky ribs dripping with a rich, tomato-tinged homemade sauce; infused with exotic nuances of pineapple, soy sauce, and ginger; rubbed down with an eye-opening Cajun spice blend; or kissed with the gentle sweetness of maple syrup. Come see us at Allrecipes.com to explore new renditions of all your old favorites.

about the recipes

Half the fun of an Allrecipes recipe is the story behind it - each of our recipes has comments submitted by the contributor to help explain how the recipe came about, what it's like, or how they use it. As the editors of the Allrecipes cookbooks, both online and in print, the staff works hard to preserve the character of the contributed recipe, but also strives to ensure consistency, accuracy, and completeness in the published version and throughout the collection.

all in the timing

At the top right corner of every recipe in the book, you'll find "Preparation," "Cooking," and "Ready In" times. These times are approximate! Depending on whether you let the butcher do the cutting for you, how much time you really have to let the marinade soak in, how high you pile the charcoal, and any number of other factors - you may find that it takes less or more time than what we've estimated. The "Ready In" times will tell you, on average, how much time the recipe takes from start to finish. With many barbeque and grilling recipes, this will be longer than the "Preparation" time plus the "Cooking" time. These are recipes that contain intermediate steps that aren't prepping or cooking, such as marinating meat. Refer to the "Ready In" time to know roughly how long you need between opening the book and serving the finished dish to an appreciative crowd.

need help? we're here for you!

Need more information about an unfamiliar ingredient or cooking term, general cooking information, or difficult techniques? We've got a whole section of Allrecipes.com dedicated to giving you all the help you need. In our Advice section, you can search for thousands of kitchen terms, follow photo-filled step-by-step tutorials to learn important cooking skills, and browse or search hundreds of articles that will help you decide what to make and teach you how to make it. You can access all this information at Allrecipes.com by clicking the "Advice" tab at the top of any page on the site, or by going to this address:

http://allrecipes.com/advice/

beyond the book

Each of the recipes in this book can be accessed online at Allrecipes.com. The online versions have some handy, whiz-bang features we didn't manage to squeeze into this book. If you'd like to adjust the number of servings for a recipe, view detailed nutritional information, convert the measurements to metric, or email a copy to a friend, it's all just a click away! The online version also includes user reviews that often include variations and handy tips. We've created a special place on Allrecipes.com where you can find any recipe in this book simply by entering its page number. Check it out!

http://allrecipes.com/tnt/grillingbbq/page.asp

your two cents

Once you try a recipe in this book, you can tell the rest of the world all about it! First, locate the recipe on Allrecipes.com (see above). Next, click on the link that says, "Add to Recipe Box" (to the right of the recipe's ingredient list). Then, follow the instructions to set up a FREE recipe box of your own. Once you've added the recipe to your box, you can rate it on a scale of 1 to 5 stars and share your comments with the millions of other people who use the site. Come tell us what you think!

tried and true

If you'd like to find out more about this book, the recipes, and other Allrecipes "tried and true" cookbooks - join us online at **http://allrecipes.com/tnt/** or send us an email at **tnt@allrecipes.com**

sauces, marinades and rubs

It could be a quick sprinkling of spice rub, a long soak in a marinade with that perfect balance of sweet, sour, and savory, or a distinctive dipping and basting sauce to grace freshly grilled meats and vegetables with flavor. Spices and sauces are what give your grilled foods their unique character; turning the very same piece of meat into fajitas, satay, jerk, tandoori, teriyaki, or souvlaki.

Jim Goode's BBQ Beef Rub

Submitted by: **Martha**

Makes: ¾ cup

Preparation: 15 minutes

Ready In: 15 minutes

"This beef rub is great for beef, pork and lamb. Once you mix the spices they'll keep about 4 months in an airtight jar. When ready to use, just rub into the meat, wrap in plastic, and refrigerate the night before grilling."

INGREDIENTS

2½ tablespoons dark brown sugar

2 tablespoons paprika

2 teaspoons mustard powder

2 teaspoons onion powder

2 teaspoons garlic powder

1½ teaspoons dried basil

1 teaspoon ground bay leaves

¾ teaspoon ground coriander seed

¾ teaspoon ground savory

¾ teaspoon dried thyme

¾ teaspoon ground black pepper

¾ teaspoon ground white pepper

⅛ teaspoon ground cumin

salt to taste

DIRECTIONS

1. In a small bowl, mix together the brown sugar, paprika, mustard powder, onion powder, garlic powder, basil, bay leaves, coriander, savory, thyme, black pepper, white pepper, cumin, and salt. Store in an airtight jar at room temperature until ready to use.

Dry Rub for Ribs

Submitted by: **Denise Smith**

Makes: ½ cup

Preparation: 10 minutes

Ready In: 10 minutes

"Here's a super simple dry rub for a slab of pork ribs. Works great with chicken, too."

INGREDIENTS

3 tablespoons brown sugar

1½ tablespoons paprika

1½ tablespoons salt

1½ tablespoons ground black pepper

1 teaspoon garlic powder

DIRECTIONS

1. Mix together the brown sugar, paprika, salt, black pepper, and garlic powder. Rub into pork ribs. For best results, allow ribs to marinate overnight. Grill ribs as desired.

BBQ Dry Rub

Submitted by: **Cindy**

Makes: 3¹/₂ cups

Preparation: 10 minutes

Ready In: 10 minutes

"My family has been making this dry rub for years. It is awesome on country-style ribs and pork steaks!"

INGREDIENTS

1¹/₄ cups white sugar

1¹/₄ cups brown sugar

¹/₂ cup salt

¹/₄ cup freshly ground black pepper

¹/₄ cup paprika

DIRECTIONS

1. In a medium bowl, mix together white and brown sugars, salt, pepper, and paprika. Rub onto pork 10 minutes prior to grilling. Store any leftover rub in a sealed container.

Hugh's Dry Rub

Submitted by: **Hugh**

Makes: 2 cups

Preparation: 15 minutes

Ready In: 15 minutes

"Use this dry rub on your favorite meat before grilling. It stores well in an airtight container, and I've had a lot of positive feedback no matter what I cook it on."

INGREDIENTS

1/2 cup paprika

3 tablespoons cayenne pepper

5 tablespoons freshly ground black pepper

6 tablespoons garlic powder

3 tablespoons onion powder

6 tablespoons salt

2 1/2 tablespoons dried oregano

2 1/2 tablespoons dried thyme

DIRECTIONS

1. In a medium bowl, combine the paprika, cayenne pepper, ground black pepper, garlic powder, onion powder, salt, oregano, and thyme. Mix well, and store in a cool, dry place in an airtight container.

Jerk Seasoning

Submitted by: **Celia**

Makes: ¼ cup

Preparation: 10 minutes

Ready In: 10 minutes

"This is a great seasoning for any meat. You can make more of it all at once and store it in an airtight container. Make sure you store it in a cool, dry place."

INGREDIENTS

2 tablespoons dried minced onion

2½ teaspoons dried thyme

2 teaspoons ground allspice

2 teaspoons ground black pepper

½ teaspoon ground cinnamon

½ teaspoon cayenne pepper

½ teaspoon salt

2 tablespoons vegetable oil

DIRECTIONS

1. In a small bowl, stir together the dried onion, thyme, allspice, ground black pepper, cinnamon, cayenne pepper, and salt. Coat meat lightly with oil, then rub seasoning onto meat.

Fajita Marinade I

Submitted by: **Roberta Haferkamp**

Makes: 2 cups

Preparation: 15 minutes

Ready In: 15 minutes

"Delicious fajita marinade made with lime juice, olive oil, and soy sauce, and spiced up with cayenne and black pepper. Makes enough marinade for 2 pounds of meat."

INGREDIENTS

1/4 cup lime juice

1/3 cup water

2 tablespoons olive oil

4 cloves garlic, crushed

2 teaspoons soy sauce

1 teaspoon salt

1/2 teaspoon liquid smoke flavoring

1/2 teaspoon cayenne pepper

1/2 teaspoon ground black pepper

DIRECTIONS

1. In a large resealable plastic bag, mix together the lime juice, water, olive oil, garlic, soy sauce, salt, and liquid smoke flavoring. Stir in cayenne and black pepper.

2. Place desired meat in the marinade, and refrigerate at least 2 hours, or overnight. Cook as desired.

Super Fajita Marinade

Submitted by: **Susan Wickstrom**

Makes: ¾ cup

Preparation: 15 minutes

Ready In: 12 hours 15 minutes

"This is best when prepared a day ahead. Makes zesty flavorful fajitas every time. Great for beef OR chicken."

INGREDIENTS

3 limes, juiced

2 green onions, chopped

3 cloves garlic, minced

3 tablespoons chopped fresh cilantro

2 tablespoons vegetable oil

1/2 teaspoon red pepper flakes

1/4 teaspoon ground coriander

1/4 teaspoon ground anise seed (optional)

DIRECTIONS

1. In a medium bowl, combine the lime juice, green onions, garlic, cilantro, oil, red pepper, coriander, and anise. Whisk until well blended.

2. Pour mixture over your favorite meat, cover, and marinate for 12 to 24 hours before cooking as desired.

Sweet Balsamic Marinade

Submitted by: **Lol**

Makes: 1¹/₂ cups

Preparation: 10 minutes

Ready In: 10 minutes

"This slightly sweet marinade is perfect for chicken and other poultry. If you boil any leftover marinade for a few minutes it makes a great sauce!"

INGREDIENTS

³/₄ cup balsamic vinegar

¹/₂ cup olive oil

2 teaspoons brown sugar

¹/₄ cup finely minced sweet onion

cracked black pepper

DIRECTIONS

1. In a small bowl, whisk together the vinegar, oil, brown sugar, onion, and pepper. Pour over desired meat, and marinate in the refrigerator for 1 to 4 hours, turning meat occasionally.

Zesty Barbeque Marinade

Submitted by: **Block**

Makes: 2 1/2 cups

Preparation: 10 minutes

Ready In: 10 minutes

"This zesty marinade is fit for any barbeque. It leaves meat tender and extra juicy with a little kick after each bite. Whiskey and habanero sauce create a little spark that's hard to extinguish. For a little sweetness, add 2 tablespoons molasses to the mixture."

INGREDIENTS

1 cup barbeque sauce

1/2 cup steak sauce

1/2 (12 fluid ounce) can or bottle beer

1/2 cup bourbon whiskey

3 tablespoons Worcestershire sauce

2 tablespoons crushed garlic

2 tablespoons seasoned salt

2 tablespoons ground black pepper

2 tablespoons dried minced onion

1 tablespoon dried basil

1 tablespoon dried oregano

2 tablespoons habanero hot sauce

3 teaspoons curry powder

2 tablespoons red pepper flakes

2 tablespoons brown sugar

DIRECTIONS

1. In a large bowl, mix together the barbeque sauce, steak sauce, beer, bourbon whiskey, Worcestershire sauce, garlic, seasoned salt, black pepper, dried onion, basil, oregano, habanero hot sauce, curry powder, red pepper flakes, and brown sugar.

2. Cover the bottom of a 9x13 inch baking dish with approximately ½ the marinade. Place desired meat in the dish, and cover with remaining mixture. Cover, and marinate in the refrigerator at least 6 hours before grilling as desired.

Cornell Chicken Marinade

Submitted by: **Kathy**

Makes: 3 cups

Preparation: 10 minutes

Ready In: 24 hours 10 minutes

"A lovely chicken marinade with oil, vinegar, poultry seasoning, egg and salt and pepper. Your chicken will love you for this baste, and so will the family."

INGREDIENTS

1 egg

1 cup vegetable oil

2 cups cider vinegar

3 tablespoons salt

1 tablespoon poultry seasoning

1 teaspoon ground black pepper

DIRECTIONS

1. Crack the egg into a medium bowl and whisk until beaten. Slowly whisk in the oil until fully blended. Then whisk in the vinegar, salt, poultry seasoning, and ground black pepper. Set some of the sauce aside to use for basting while grilling. Place chicken in shallow baking dish, and coat with sauce. Cover, and marinate in the refrigerator for 24 hours.

Kabob Marinade

Submitted by: **Jon Devore**

Makes: 3 cups

Preparation: 15 minutes

Ready In: 4 hours 15 minutes

"This is a tasty, easy to make marinade that is great for any grilled meat. It makes enough for about two pounds of uncooked meat. Hunters - try this on your deer."

INGREDIENTS

1 cup vegetable oil

3/4 cup soy sauce

1/2 cup lemon juice

1/4 cup Worcestershire sauce

1/4 cup prepared mustard

11/2 teaspoons coarsely cracked black pepper

2 cloves garlic, minced

1 teaspoon meat tenderizer (optional)

DIRECTIONS

1. In a large resealable plastic bag, combine the oil, soy sauce, lemon juice, Worcestershire sauce, mustard, ground black pepper, garlic, and meat tenderizer. Mix well, and add your favorite meat. Seal the bag, and marinate in the refrigerator for 4 to 24 hours.

Marinade for Chicken

Submitted by: **Jill**

Makes: 4 cups

Preparation: 10 minutes

Ready In: 10 minutes

"A delicious barbecue sauce for chicken on the grill. My father has used this since I can remember, and he always receives the compliments at mealtime."

INGREDIENTS

1¹/₂ cups vegetable oil

³/₄ cup soy sauce

¹/₂ cup Worcestershire sauce

¹/₂ cup red wine vinegar

¹/₃ cup lemon juice

2 tablespoons dry mustard

1 teaspoon salt

1 tablespoon black pepper

1¹/₂ teaspoons finely minced fresh parsley

DIRECTIONS

1. In a medium bowl, mix together oil, soy sauce, Worcestershire sauce, wine vinegar, and lemon juice. Stir in mustard powder, salt, pepper, and parsley. Use to marinate chicken before cooking as desired. The longer you marinate, the more flavor it will have.

Chicken and Turkey Marinade

Submitted by: **Elaine Maxwell**

Makes: 5 cups

Preparation: 15 minutes

Ready In: 45 minutes

"A 24 hour marinade, guaranteed to please every time. Chicken or turkey is always moist, and tender. Use half of a recipe for a chicken, or the full recipe for a turkey of up to 25 pounds. Everyone will clamor for this recipe!!! Use the drippings from the pan to make gravy as usual. It is not necessary to strain drippings first."

INGREDIENTS

1 cup olive oil

1/2 cup soy sauce

4 lemons, juiced

1/4 cup prepared yellow mustard

1/4 cup minced fresh chives

1/2 cup minced fresh sage

1/2 cup minced fresh oregano

1/2 cup chopped fresh parsley

1/4 cup minced fresh thyme

2 teaspoons minced garlic, or to taste

1 tablespoon paprika

3 tablespoons salt-free herb seasoning blend

DIRECTIONS

1. In a small bowl, whisk together the olive oil, soy sauce, lemon juice, and mustard. Stir in chives, sage, oregano, parsley, thyme, garlic, paprika, and herb seasoning. Cover, and refrigerate for 30 minutes to allow flavors to blend before marinating your favorite meat.

2. Place turkey or chicken in a 30 gallon plastic kitchen bag. Pour marinade over the bird. Grasp the bag a few inches above the poultry, and press air from the bag. Seal with a twist tie. Rotate bag to coat turkey with the marinade. Marinate in the refrigerator 24 hours, repositioning the bag every 4 hours, or so. Remove poultry from bag before roasting, and transfer marinade to a saucepan. Boil marinade for a few minutes, then use to baste the turkey every 30 minutes, or so, while roasting. Discard any remaining marinade when turkey is done.

Marinade for Steak I

Submitted by: **K a t**

Makes: 2 cups

Preparation: 10 minutes

Ready In: 10 minutes

"This here's a great marinade for any cut of beef, but I like to use it on steak. It contains basic ingredients that, when combined and allowed to blend, will give you a tender, juicy piece of meat every time."

INGREDIENTS

1 cup vegetable oil

1/2 cup soy sauce

1/3 cup red wine vinegar

1/4 cup fresh lemon juice

3 tablespoons Worcestershire sauce

1 tablespoon freshly ground black pepper

2 tablespoons Dijon-style prepared mustard

1 onion, sliced

2 cloves garlic, minced

DIRECTIONS

1. In a medium bowl, combine the oil, soy sauce, vinegar, lemon juice, Worcestershire sauce, ground black pepper, mustard, onion, and garlic. Mix together well, and use to marinate your favorite meat.

Doreen's Steak Marinade

Submitted by: **Doreen**

Makes: 1¹/₄ cups
Preparation: 10 minutes
Ready In: 10 minutes

"This is one of my favorite marinades when we eat red meat!"

INGREDIENTS

¹/₃ cup sherry

¹/₃ cup soy sauce

¹/₃ cup vegetable oil

2 tablespoons honey

2 tablespoons grated fresh ginger root

1 clove garlic, minced

DIRECTIONS

1. In a medium bowl, mix sherry, soy sauce, vegetable oil, honey, ginger, and garlic. Marinate steaks for at least 4 hours before grilling as desired.

Absolutely Ultimate Marinade

Submitted by: **Minnesotamom**

Makes: 2 cups

Preparation: 10 minutes

Cooking: 5 minutes

Ready In: 15 minutes

"This has been the secret recipe in my family for years. All of our guests rave about it! The only downfall is that we always wind up hosting! This works great with chicken and steak. Try some of each."

INGREDIENTS

2 tablespoons sesame seeds

1 bunch green onions, chopped

8 cloves garlic, minced

2 tablespoons tahini

1/2 cup soy sauce

1/2 cup white sugar

1/4 cup red wine vinegar

1/2 teaspoon freshly ground black pepper

DIRECTIONS

1. Place the sesame seeds in a dry skillet over medium heat. Cook and stir for 5 minutes, or until golden brown and fragrant.

2. In a medium bowl, mix toasted sesame seeds, green onions, garlic, tahini, soy sauce, white sugar, red wine vinegar, and pepper. Place desired meat in the mixture, cover, and marinate as long as you like, but overnight is best. Grill as desired.

Korean Marinade

Submitted by: **Curlie**

Makes: ¾ cup

Preparation: 10 minutes

Ready In: 10 minutes

"This is a great marinade for beef short ribs, chicken, or steak. Serve with steamed rice, beer, and kim chee."

INGREDIENTS

6 tablespoons soy sauce

3 tablespoons white sugar

2 tablespoons sesame oil

1 green onion, chopped

1 clove garlic, minced

2 tablespoons toasted sesame seeds

1 tablespoon all-purpose flour

1 pinch ground black pepper

DIRECTIONS

1. In a medium bowl, mix together the soy sauce, sugar, sesame oil, green onion, garlic, toasted sesame seeds, flour, and pepper. Place meat in the marinade, cover, and refrigerate for 30 minutes, or overnight.

Korean BBQ Chicken Marinade

Submitted by: **So Il-Byung**

Makes: 3 cups

Preparation: 10 minutes

Cooking: 15 minutes

Ready In: 25 minutes

"This sauce is from the very popular 'chicken bowls' in my hometown. It's very tasty! Use it as a marinade for chicken, or to baste chicken while grilling. Increase the hot chile paste as desired. Four tablespoons is usually as much as anyone can take!"

INGREDIENTS

1 cup white sugar

1 cup soy sauce

1 cup water

1 teaspoon onion powder

1 teaspoon ground ginger

1 tablespoon lemon juice (optional)

4 teaspoons hot chile paste (optional)

DIRECTIONS

1. In a medium saucepan over high heat, whisk together the sugar, soy sauce, water, onion powder, and ground ginger. Bring to a boil. Reduce heat to low, and simmer 5 minutes.

2. Remove the mixture from heat, cool, and whisk in lemon juice and hot chile paste. Place chicken in the mixture. Cover, and marinate in the refrigerator at least 4 hours before preparing chicken as desired.

Teriyaki Marinade I

Submitted by: **Tim Bond**

Makes: 9 cups

Preparation: 10 minutes

Cooking: 1 hour 10 minutes

Ready In: 1 hour 40 minutes

"In addition to his duties as Associate Artistic Director for the Oregon Shakespeare Festival, Tim is head chef for staff BBQ's. The secret to his magic is a sweet teriyaki that is a wonderful marinade and basting sauce. Use for everything from salmon to chicken to eggplant. It even works for tofu. This recipe makes enough for a whole salmon."

INGREDIENTS

1/3 cup grated fresh ginger

1/3 cup minced garlic

1 1/2 cups dry vermouth, divided

5 cups soy sauce

1 cup honey, or as needed

1 3/4 cups oyster sauce

DIRECTIONS

1. In a large saucepan, combine ginger, garlic, and 1 cup vermouth. Bring to a boil over medium heat, and cook until ginger and garlic are tender.

2. Stir in remaining vermouth, soy sauce, honey, and oyster sauce. Bring to a low boil, and reduce heat to low. Simmer for 15 minutes to 1 hour; longer is better, but 15 minutes will do in a pinch. Watch carefully to be sure that the mixture does not foam and boil over.

3. Remove marinade from heat, and taste. The sauce should be sweet, not salty. If necessary, add up to 1 more cup of honey. Cool to room temperature. Marinade can be refrigerated for 4 to 5 days.

Teriyaki Marinade

Submitted by: **Mary Savard**

Makes: 3 cups

Preparation: 10 minutes

Ready In: 10 minutes

"Marinate chicken, steaks, or other favorite meats in this marinade for at least 2 hours before grilling. Enjoy!"

INGREDIENTS

1 cup soy sauce

1 cup water

3/4 cup white sugar

1/4 cup Worcestershire sauce

3 tablespoons distilled white vinegar

3 tablespoons vegetable oil

1/3 cup dried onion flakes

2 teaspoons garlic powder

1 teaspoon grated fresh ginger

DIRECTIONS

1. In a medium bowl, mix the soy sauce, water, sugar, Worcestershire sauce, vinegar, oil, onions, garlic powder, and ginger. Stir together until sugar dissolves. Voila - marinade!

Teriyaki Marinade III

Submitted by: **Denyse**

Makes: 1 cup

Preparation: 10 minutes

Ready In: 10 minutes

"Easy and wonderful teriyaki marinade for barbeque or roasting. For a zestier marinade, use lime or lemon juice; for a milder version, use water. If you would like to use the marinade as a sauce, you can boil it after removing the meat and add a little slurry of cornstarch and warm water to thicken it. When I make the sauce, I usually add some sesame seeds for looks. You can add fresh or ground ginger if you like, too."

INGREDIENTS

1/2 cup soy sauce

1/4 cup packed brown sugar

1/2 cup orange juice

1 clove garlic, minced

1 teaspoon ground black pepper (optional)

DIRECTIONS

1. In a small bowl, stir together soy sauce, brown sugar, orange juice, garlic, and pepper. Pour over beef, pork, or chicken. Cover, and marinate in the refrigerator for 4 hours, or overnight. The longer the meat is marinated, the stronger the flavor will be.

Basic Brine for Smoking Meat

Submitted by: **Smokin' Ron**

Makes: 1 quart

Preparation: 10 minutes

Ready In: 10 minutes

"This is a very basic brine recipe for preparing meats and fish for smoking. Add any personal taste preferences to the brine for additional flavor enhancement. I like to add white wine, soy sauce, and various herbs and spices. Anything that you like will work, so experiment at will."

INGREDIENTS

¼ cup kosher salt

¼ cup packed brown sugar

4 cups water

DIRECTIONS

1. In a medium bowl, combine the salt, sugar and water. Whisk vigorously until all the salt and sugar is dissolved. Then pour this mixture over the meat, poultry, or fish that you are preparing. Soak for several hours, or overnight. (Note: Make certain the meat is fully submerged in the brine, and make more brine as needed to fully cover the meat.)

Blackberry BBQ Sauce

Submitted by: **Ina James Point**

Makes: 2 cups sauce

Preparation: 10 minutes

Ready In: 10 minutes

"Sweet and fruity basting sauce that will have your guests clamoring for your 'secret.' It is an especially good sauce for pork or beef ribs."

INGREDIENTS

1/2 cup blackberry preserves

11/2 cups ketchup

1/8 cup brown sugar

1/8 teaspoon cayenne pepper

1/4 teaspoon mustard powder

2 tablespoons red wine vinegar

DIRECTIONS

1. In a medium bowl, mix together blackberry preserves, ketchup, brown sugar, cayenne pepper, mustard powder, and red wine vinegar. Use to baste pork or beef ribs while grilling.

Devil's Steak Sauce

Submitted by: **Bernard Montgomerie**

Makes: ½ cup

Preparation: 10 minutes

Cooking: 15 minutes

Ready In: 25 minutes

"A brilliant steak sauce that really brings out the flavor of any type of grilled steak. It's best with eye fillet or Scotch steaks. Raspberry jam is the wildly inventive twist that really makes this sauce unique."

INGREDIENTS

2 tablespoons raspberry jam

2 tablespoons brown sugar

2 tablespoons Worcestershire sauce

2 tablespoons tomato sauce

2 tablespoons malt vinegar

5 drops hot pepper sauce

salt and freshly ground black pepper to taste

DIRECTIONS

1. In a saucepan over high heat, blend raspberry jam, brown sugar, Worcestershire sauce, tomato sauce, malt vinegar, hot pepper sauce, salt, and pepper. Bring to a boil over high heat, reduce heat to low, and simmer 10 minutes, or until thickened.

Rockin' Baby Back Ribs Sauce

Submitted by: **Holly**

Makes: 2 cups

Preparation: 15 minutes

Cooking: 5 hours

Ready In: 5 hours 45 minutes

"This is a watermelon based barbecue sauce that is very similar to a recipe used at a well known restaurant. Great for baby back ribs! You can either serve this sauce on the side, or baste the ribs with it while you barbecue them."

INGREDIENTS

6 pounds seedless watermelon

1 (6 ounce) can tomato paste

1 tablespoon onion powder

1 tablespoon garlic powder

2 cups firmly packed brown sugar

1/2 cup dry sherry

2 teaspoons lemon juice

1 teaspoon liquid smoke flavoring

DIRECTIONS

1. Cut the melon flesh into chunks, and discard the rind. Place the chunks in a large saucepan over medium heat for 2 to 3 hours, stirring occasionally, or until the melon is the consistency of applesauce.

2. Stir in the tomato paste, onion powder, garlic powder, brown sugar, sherry, lemon juice, and liquid smoke. Reduce heat to low, and simmer uncovered for 2 hours. Allow mixture to cool to room temperature before using.

Applesauce Barbeque Sauce

Submitted by: **Cheryl**

Makes: 3 1/2 cups

Preparation: 10 minutes

Cooking: 20 minutes

Ready In: 30 minutes

"Applesauce gives this sauce a nice thick texture that coats well on meat. It has a sweet spicy flavor that is excellent on chicken or pork. It may also be canned in sterile containers for later use, or for giving as gifts."

INGREDIENTS

1 cup applesauce

1/2 cup ketchup

2 cups unpacked brown sugar

6 tablespoons lemon juice

1/2 teaspoon salt

1/2 teaspoon ground black pepper

1/2 teaspoon paprika

1/2 teaspoon garlic powder

1/2 teaspoon ground cinnamon

DIRECTIONS

1. In a saucepan over medium heat, mix applesauce, ketchup, brown sugar, lemon juice, salt, pepper, paprika, garlic powder, and cinnamon. Bring mixture to a boil. Remove from heat, and cool completely. Use to baste the meat of your choice.

Barbeque Sauce II

Submitted by: **Sue Theiss**

Makes: 6 cups

Preparation: 10 minutes

Ready In: 10 minutes

"A different kind of honey barbeque sauce that goes well with any meat."

INGREDIENTS

2 (18 ounce) bottles honey barbeque sauce

1/4 cup lemon juice

1 cup brown sugar

1/4 cup Worcestershire sauce

1/2 cup steak sauce

2 tablespoons dried onion flakes

1 (12 fluid ounce) can or bottle cola-flavored carbonated beverage

DIRECTIONS

1. In a medium bowl, mix together barbeque sauce, lemon juice, brown sugar, Worcestershire sauce, steak sauce, and onion flakes. Pour in the cola, and stir until blended.

Honey Barbecue Sauce

Submitted by: **Kimberly D**

Makes: 2 cups

Preparation: 15 minutes

Ready In: 15 minutes

*"Simple and sweet, this sauce is fantastic for ribs!!
Makes enough to baste 3 to 4 pounds worth."*

INGREDIENTS

1 cup honey

1/4 cup molasses

3 tablespoons ketchup

1/8 teaspoon ground cinnamon

1/2 teaspoon paprika

1/8 teaspoon ground ginger

1 tablespoon seasoned salt

1 tablespoon meat tenderizer

1/8 teaspoon ground black pepper

1/4 teaspoon salt

1/8 teaspoon dried oregano

1/4 teaspoon minced garlic

1/4 cup steak sauce

2 tablespoons Worcestershire sauce

1 tablespoon prepared mustard

1 1/2 cups brown sugar

DIRECTIONS

1. In a medium bowl, stir together the honey, molasses, ketchup, cinnamon, paprika, ginger, seasoned salt, meat tenderizer, ground black pepper, salt, oregano, garlic, steak sauce, Worcestershire sauce, mustard, and brown sugar until well blended.

2. Cover, and refrigerate until ready to use.

Uncle Mike's Vinegar Pepper Sauce

Submitted by: **Mike Henderlight**

Makes: 3 cups
Preparation: 10 minutes
Cooking: 15 minutes
Ready In: 35 minutes

"This is a North Carolina-style BBQ sauce that I have used for years. It's great on any meat. Lots of vinegar - that's the North Carolina way! Be careful though, this one's spicy."

INGREDIENTS

1½ cups cider vinegar

10 tablespoons ketchup

½ teaspoon cayenne pepper, or to taste

1 pinch red pepper flakes

1 tablespoon white sugar

½ cup water

salt and black pepper to taste

DIRECTIONS

1. In a small saucepan over medium heat, stir together the vinegar, ketchup, cayenne pepper, red pepper flakes, sugar, and water.

2. Simmer for 15 minutes, or until all the sugar dissolves. Season to taste with salt and pepper. Remove from heat, and let cool. Use to baste your favorite meat while grilling.

Eastern North Carolina Barbeque Sauce

Submitted by: **Lori**

Makes: 2 quarts

Preparation: 10 minutes

Ready In: 3 hours 10 minutes

"This piquant and spicy vinegar-based sauce, popular in Eastern North Carolina, is not for lightweights! It's great for all meats, but best on pork."

INGREDIENTS

2 quarts cider vinegar

1/4 cup salt

2 tablespoons cayenne pepper

3 tablespoons red pepper flakes

1 cup light brown sugar

1 tablespoon hot pepper sauce

DIRECTIONS

1. In a large bowl, mix together cider vinegar, salt, cayenne pepper, red pepper flakes, light brown sugar, and hot pepper sauce. Stir until salt and brown sugar have dissolved. Cover, and let stand at least 3 hours before using as a basting sauce or serving on meat.

Best Carolina BBQ Meat Sauce

Submitted by: **Andy Tripp**

Makes: 3 cups

Preparation: 10 minutes

Cooking: 40 minutes

Ready In: 8 hours 55 minutes

"I can't take all the credit for this stuff. I have had to search, and snoop and experiment to get it right. (Thanks Big Daddy's!) But I've had barbeque in some of the best little places in the Carolina's, and this stuff rules there! Fantastic on pork! Or try brushing some on chicken as it finishes off the grill! Use fresh ground peppers for the best flavor. This will keep in fridge for a couple of weeks."

INGREDIENTS

1½ cups prepared yellow mustard

½ cup packed brown sugar

¾ cup cider vinegar

¾ cup beer

1 tablespoon chili powder

1 teaspoon freshly ground black pepper

1 teaspoon freshly ground white pepper

½ teaspoon cayenne pepper

1½ teaspoons Worcestershire sauce

2 tablespoons butter, room temperature

1½ teaspoons liquid smoke flavoring

1 teaspoon Louisiana-style hot sauce, or to taste

DIRECTIONS

1. In a heavy non-reactive saucepan, stir together the mustard, brown sugar, vinegar, and beer. Season with chili powder and black, white, and cayenne peppers. Bring to a simmer over medium-low heat, and cook for about 20 minutes. DO NOT BOIL, or you will scorch the sugar and peppers.

2. Mix in the Worcestershire sauce, butter, and liquid smoke. Simmer for another 15 to 20 minutes. Taste, and season with hot sauce to your liking. Pour into an airtight jar, and refrigerate for overnight to allow flavors to blend. The vinegar taste may be a little strong until the sauce completely cools.

Grant's Famous Midnight Grill BBQ Sauce

Submitted by: **Grant Mosesian**

Makes: 2¹/₂ cups
Preparation: 15 minutes
Ready In: 15 minutes

"A sauce that's big, bold, and spicy. This one will keep them coming back for more."

INGREDIENTS

1 (18 ounce) bottle barbeque sauce

2 tablespoons Scotch whiskey

1¹/₂ teaspoons Worcestershire sauce

¹/₂ teaspoon ground ginger

¹/₂ teaspoon cayenne pepper

¹/₂ teaspoon paprika

¹/₂ teaspoon chili powder

¹/₂ teaspoon garlic powder

¹/₂ teaspoon onion salt

¹/₂ teaspoon dried oregano

1 tablespoon red pepper flakes

1¹/₂ tablespoons white sugar

¹/₂ teaspoon ground black pepper, or to taste

¹/₄ teaspoon hot pepper sauce, or to taste

DIRECTIONS

1. In a medium bowl, stir together the barbeque sauce, whiskey, Worcestershire sauce, ginger, cayenne pepper, paprika, chili powder, garlic powder, onion salt, oregano, red pepper flakes, sugar, ground black pepper, and hot pepper sauce. Cover, and keep refrigerated until ready to use.

Bourbon Whiskey BBQ Sauce

Submitted by: **Kevin**

Makes: 4 cups

Preparation: 15 minutes

Cooking: 30 minutes

Ready In: 45 minutes

"This is a barbecue sauce recipe using Kentucky bourbon whiskey. For best results, refrigerate for a day or two, allowing the flavors to blend."

INGREDIENTS

1/2 onion, minced

4 cloves garlic, minced

3/4 cup bourbon whiskey

1/2 teaspoon ground black pepper

1/2 tablespoon salt

2 cups ketchup

1/4 cup tomato paste

1/3 cup cider vinegar

2 tablespoons liquid smoke flavoring

1/4 cup Worcestershire sauce

1/2 cup packed brown sugar

1/3 teaspoon hot pepper sauce, or to taste

DIRECTIONS

1. In a large skillet over medium heat, combine the onion, garlic, and whiskey. Simmer for 10 minutes, or until onion is translucent. Mix in the ground black pepper, salt, ketchup, tomato paste, vinegar, liquid smoke, Worcestershire sauce, brown sugar, and hot pepper sauce.

2. Bring to a boil. Reduce heat to medium-low, and simmer for 20 minutes. Run sauce through a strainer if you prefer a smooth sauce.

Smoker Sauce

Submitted by: **Douglas J. Patrick**

Makes: 4 cups

Preparation: 15 minutes

Ready In: 15 minutes

"I came up with this sauce for my wood smoker. It works on the barbecue, as well, or even as a marinade. I like to keep this in a sealed jar in the refrigerator until I'm ready to use it."

INGREDIENTS

1 (18 ounce) bottle barbeque sauce

1/2 (8 ounce) jar salsa

1/2 cup soy sauce

3/4 cup packed brown sugar

1 teaspoon ground ginger

1 tablespoon crushed garlic

1 tablespoon coarsely ground black pepper

salt to taste

DIRECTIONS

1. In a large bowl, stir together the barbeque sauce, salsa, soy sauce, brown sugar, ginger, garlic, ground black pepper, and salt. Store in a jar in the refrigerator until ready to use. Use as a marinade or a basting sauce when smoking meats or fish.

Kathy's Award Winning Barbeque Sauce

Submitted by: **Kathy**

Makes: 2 1/2 cups

Preparation: 20 minutes

Cooking: 1 hour

Ready In: 1 hour 20 minutes

"This is a thick and spicy barbeque chicken recipe that has won several cooking contests. The sauce consists of molasses, brown sugar, tomato juice and spices all pureed together in a blender. Some may wish to cut the amount of pepper in half."

INGREDIENTS

1 cup ketchup

1 tablespoon Worcestershire sauce

1 cup molasses

2 tablespoons brown sugar

1/4 cup chopped onion

1 tablespoon garlic powder

1 teaspoon ground black pepper

1 teaspoon cayenne pepper

2 tablespoons lemon juice

1 (5.5 ounce) can tomato juice

2 tablespoons liquid smoke flavoring

DIRECTIONS

1. In a blender or food processor, combine the ketchup, Worcestershire sauce, molasses, brown sugar, onion, garlic powder, ground black pepper, cayenne pepper, lemon juice, tomato juice, and liquid smoke flavoring. Puree until smooth, and transfer to a saucepan.

2. Place saucepan on the stove over medium heat. Bring mixture to a boil, reduce heat to low, and simmer for about 1 hour, or to desired thickness.

Bubba's Best BBQ Sauce

Submitted by: **Bubba**

Makes: 3 cups

Preparation: 10 minutes

Cooking: 10 minutes

Ready In: 20 minutes

"A hot-sweet sauce that is good on just about anything. You can use any kind of cola in this recipe, just don't use diet cola. It makes the sauce bitter."

INGREDIENTS

1 cup cola-flavored carbonated beverage

1 cup canned tomato sauce

1 (6 ounce) can tomato paste

1/4 cup butter

1/2 cup Worcestershire sauce

1/2 cup packed brown sugar

1/2 cup molasses

1/2 cup cider vinegar

2 1/2 teaspoons balsamic vinegar

1 1/2 tablespoons steak sauce

1 tablespoon yellow mustard

1 tablespoon chili powder

1 teaspoon dried savory

1 teaspoon onion powder

1 teaspoon garlic salt

1 teaspoon hot pepper sauce

DIRECTIONS

1. In a large saucepan, mix together the cola, tomato sauce, tomato paste, butter, Worcestershire sauce, brown sugar, molasses, cider and balsamic vinegars, steak sauce, and mustard. Season with chili powder, savory, onion powder, garlic salt, and hot pepper sauce, and stir to blend. Cook over low heat, stirring occasionally, until the mixture is thick enough to coat the back of a metal spoon.

Bar-B-Que Sauce

Submitted by: **Debi K**

Makes: 1 cup

Preparation: 10 minutes

Cooking: 10 minutes

Ready In: 30 minutes

"This is an easy to make Bar-B-Que sauce using ingredients most people have at home."

INGREDIENTS

1/2 cup ketchup

2 tablespoons brown sugar

2 tablespoons Worcestershire sauce

1 tablespoon cider vinegar

1 dash hot pepper sauce

1 teaspoon garlic powder

1/4 teaspoon mustard powder

1/4 teaspoon salt

DIRECTIONS

1. In a small saucepan over medium heat, stir together the ketchup, brown sugar, Worcestershire sauce, vinegar, hot pepper sauce, garlic powder, mustard powder, and salt. Bring to a simmer, then remove from heat and allow to cool slightly before brushing on your favorite meat.

beef and lamb

A slab of red meat with dark grill lines sizzled into a surface that gives way to blushing, juicy tenderness represents the pinnacle of eating pleasure. Ground beef—cheap, quick-cooking, and crowd-pleasing is taken for granted at a cookout, but a carefully crafted, lovingly grilled burger is a revelation. And lamb's distinctive flavor is never more luscious than when it's been touched by sear and smoke.

Blake's Best Steak

Submitted by: **Blake**

Makes: 4 servings

Preparation: 15 minutes

Cooking: 15 minutes

Ready In: 45 minutes

"A very flavorful steak as good as the ones you pay $30 for in the restaurants. Serve with sauteed mushrooms and a baked potato."

INGREDIENTS

4 (6 ounce) rib-eye steaks

2 tablespoons olive oil

salt and freshly ground black
   pepper to taste

8 cloves garlic, minced

4 sprigs fresh rosemary

DIRECTIONS

1. Preheat grill for high heat.

2. Rub each steak lightly with olive oil - this is to ensure that the steaks don't stick to the grill. Season with salt and pepper. Rub fresh garlic into both sides of each steak. Let stand for 15 minutes.

3. Place the steaks on the preheated grill, and immediately turn after 30 seconds (this first turn is to ensure that one side is seared). Place the fresh rosemary sprigs on top. Cook 7 minutes per side, to desired doneness, remembering to remove the rosemary sprigs before turning, and to replace on top of the meat after turning.

BBQ Steak

Submitted by: **Silau**

Makes: 6 servings

Preparation: 15 minutes

Cooking: 15 minutes

Ready In: 3 hours 30 minutes

"This recipe will give the most tasteful and delicious steak that you can ever imagine."

INGREDIENTS

1 small onion, chopped

7 cloves garlic

1/2 cup olive oil

1/2 cup vinegar

1/2 cup soy sauce

2 tablespoons chopped fresh rosemary

2 tablespoons Dijon-style prepared mustard

2 teaspoons salt

1 teaspoon black pepper

1 (2 pound) tri-tip steak

DIRECTIONS

1. Place onion, garlic, olive oil, vinegar, soy sauce, rosemary, mustard, salt, and pepper into the bowl of a food processor. Process until smooth. Place steak in a large resealable plastic bag. Pour marinade over steaks, seal, and refrigerate for about 3 hours.

2. Preheat the grill for high heat.

3. Brush grill grate with oil. Discard marinade, and place steak on the prepared grill. Cook for 7 minutes per side, or to desired doneness.

Smothered Filet Mignon

Submitted by: **Linda VanHoose**

Makes: 4 servings

Preparation: 15 minutes

Cooking: 15 minutes

Ready In: 1 hour

"A great combination of flavors. Serve with some mashed garlic red potatoes and sweetened green beans for a fabulous special occasion meal. Don't forget to serve a bottle of Cabernet or Zinfandel."

INGREDIENTS

4 (6 ounce) filet mignon steaks

seasoned salt to taste

cracked black pepper to taste

1/4 cup extra virgin olive oil

1/4 cup balsamic vinegar

1 tablespoon Dijon mustard

2 teaspoons dried rosemary

1 tablespoon butter

2 cups onion slices

1 teaspoon white sugar

4 ounces blue cheese, crumbled

DIRECTIONS

1. Season steaks with seasoned salt and black pepper, and arrange in a single layer in a large baking dish. In a bowl, whisk together olive oil, balsamic vinegar, mustard, and rosemary. Pour mixture over filets, and turn to coat. Marinate for up to 30 minutes.

2. While you are marinating the meat, melt the butter in a skillet over medium heat. Cook onion slices in butter until soft, then stir in sugar. Continue cooking until onions are caramelized. Set aside.

3. Preheat grill for high heat on one side, and medium heat on the other side.

4. Lightly oil the grill grate. Place steaks on the hot side of the grill, and cook for 10 minutes, turning once. When the steaks are almost done, move to the cooler side of the grill. Top each filet with a quarter of the caramelized onions and blue cheese. Close the lid, and continue cooking until the cheese is melted.

Savory Garlic Marinated Steaks

Submitted by: **Angie Zayac**

Makes: 2 servings
Preparation: 15 minutes
Cooking: 15 minutes
Ready In: 24 hours 30 minutes

"This beautiful marinade adds an exquisite flavor to these already tender steaks. The final result will be so tender and juicy, it will melt in your mouth."

INGREDIENTS

1/2 cup balsamic vinegar

1/4 cup soy sauce

3 tablespoons minced garlic

2 tablespoons honey

2 tablespoons olive oil

2 teaspoons ground black pepper

1 teaspoon Worcestershire sauce

1 teaspoon onion powder

1/2 teaspoon salt

1/2 teaspoon liquid smoke flavoring

1 pinch cayenne pepper

2 (1/2 pound) rib-eye steaks

DIRECTIONS

1. In a medium bowl, mix the vinegar, soy sauce, garlic, honey, olive oil, ground black pepper, Worcestershire sauce, onion powder, salt, liquid smoke, and cayenne pepper.

2. Place steaks in a shallow glass dish with the marinade, and turn to coat. For optimum flavor, rub the liquid into the meat. Cover, and marinate in the refrigerator for 1 to 2 days.

3. Preheat grill for medium-high to high heat.

4. Lightly oil the grill grate. Grill steaks 7 minutes per side, or to desired doneness. Discard leftover marinade.

Marinated Rib-eyes

Submitted by: **Della**

Makes: 4 servings

Preparation: 10 minutes

Cooking: 15 minutes

Ready In: 1 hour 25 minutes

*"Actually, this is an excellent marinade for any steak.
The marinade mainly consists of Worcestershire sauce
and brown sugar. The sugar makes the steaks tender and
gives just a hint of sweetness. I sometimes add some
Dijon mustard or red pepper flakes for a little zing."*

INGREDIENTS

4 (1/2 pound) rib-eye steaks

garlic powder to taste

onion powder to taste

salt and pepper to taste

1¾ cups Worcestershire sauce

⅓ cup brown sugar

DIRECTIONS

1. Season the steaks with the garlic powder, onion powder, salt, and pepper, and set aside.

2. Pour the Worcestershire sauce and brown sugar into a large resealable plastic bag, seal, and shake to mix. Pour half of the marinade into another large resealable bag. Place two steaks in each bag, and turn to coat. Squeeze out excess air, and seal the bags. Refrigerate for at least 1 hour.

3. Preheat grill for high heat. Drain the marinade from the steaks into a small saucepan, and bring to a boil; boil for several minutes.

4. Brush grill grate with oil. Grill steaks 7 minutes per side, to desired doneness. Baste often with the boiled marinade during the final 5 minutes of cook time.

Beer Steak

Submitted by: **Renee Thayn**

Makes: 4 servings

Preparation: 10 minutes

Cooking: 10 minutes

Ready In: 2 hours 20 minutes

"Grilled steak with a simple beer marinade!"

INGREDIENTS

4 (1/2 pound) rib-eye steaks, or
  steak of choice

2 tablespoons sea salt

2 tablespoons lemon pepper

2 (12 fluid ounce) cans or bottles beer
  of choice

DIRECTIONS

1. Place the steaks in a large, shallow container with a lid. Season each side of the steaks with the salt and lemon pepper. Gently pour the beer over the steaks (making sure the seasoning doesn't wash off). Cover, and refrigerate for 1 to 2 hours.

2. Preheat grill for high heat.

3. Lightly oil grill grate. Place steaks on grill, and discard beer marinade. Cook for 5 minutes per side, or to desired doneness.

Beer and Brown Sugar Steak Marinade

Submitted by: **Craig Jones**

Makes: 4 servings

Preparation: 30 minutes

Cooking: 15 minutes

Ready In: 1 hour 10 minutes

"I concocted this marinade on a lark and it turned out great. The flavors complement and do not overwhelm the natural taste of beef."

INGREDIENTS

2 (16 ounce) beef sirloin steaks

1/4 cup dark beer

2 tablespoons teriyaki sauce

2 tablespoons brown sugar

1/2 teaspoon seasoned salt

1/2 teaspoon black pepper

1/2 teaspoon garlic powder

DIRECTIONS

1. Preheat grill for high heat.

2. Use a fork to poke holes all over the surface of the steaks, and place steaks in a large baking dish. In a bowl, mix together beer, teriyaki sauce, and brown sugar. Pour sauce over steaks, and let sit about 5 minutes. Sprinkle with 1/2 the seasoned salt, pepper, and garlic powder; set aside for 10 minutes. Turn steaks over, sprinkle with remaining seasoned salt, pepper, and garlic powder, and continue marinating for 10 more minutes.

3. Remove steaks from marinade. Pour marinade into a small saucepan, bring to a boil, and cook for several minutes.

4. Lightly oil the grill grate. Grill steaks for 7 minutes per side, or to desired doneness. During the last few minutes of grilling, baste steaks with boiled marinade to enhance the flavor and ensure juiciness.

Steak Tip Marinade

Submitted by: **Deanna**

Makes: 8 servings

Preparation: 15 minutes

Cooking: 10 minutes

Ready In: 1 hour 25 minutes

"It took many experiments for this one. I have finally perfected a marinade that will make your mouth thirst for more."

INGREDIENTS

1/2 cup Worcestershire sauce

1 cup Italian-style salad dressing

2 teaspoons garlic pepper seasoning

1 cup barbeque sauce

2 pounds beef sirloin tip steaks

DIRECTIONS

1. In a medium bowl, mix the Worcestershire sauce, Italian-style salad dressing, garlic pepper seasoning, and barbeque sauce. Place the meat in the marinade, and turn to coat. Cover, and refrigerate for at least 1 hour.

2. Preheat grill for high heat.

3. Brush grill lightly with oil to prevent sticking. Place steaks on the grill, and discard marinade. Grill steaks 10 minutes on each side, or to desired doneness.

New York Strip Chicago Style

Submitted by: **Ted**

Makes: 2 servings

Preparation: 15 minutes

Cooking: 10 minutes

Ready In: 1 hour 25 minutes

"New York Strip on a grill has never been easier. This recipe is easy and ingredients are usually around the house!"

INGREDIENTS

1 tablespoon extra virgin olive oil

1 clove garlic, minced

1/2 teaspoon ground cinnamon

1/2 teaspoon white sugar

2 tablespoons apricot preserves

2 (1/2 pound) New York strip steaks, 1 inch thick

salt and pepper to taste

DIRECTIONS

1. In a shallow glass dish, mix the olive oil, garlic, cinnamon, sugar, and apricot preserves. Mix well, as the preserves tend to stick until warm.

2. With a knife, make several shallow slashes in both sides of the steaks. Sprinkle with salt and pepper. Place steaks in the dish with the sauce, and turn to coat. Cover with plastic wrap, and refrigerate for at least 1 hour.

3. Preheat grill for high heat.

4. Lightly oil the grill grate. Place steaks on the grill, and discard any remaining sauce. Grill steaks 10 minutes, turning occasionally, or to desired doneness.

Adobo Sirloin

Submitted by: **Tracie Commins**

Makes: 4 servings

Preparation: 15 minutes

Cooking: 12 minutes

Ready In: 2 hours 30 minutes

"Juicy top sirloin marinated in a spicy chipotle chile sauce. This meat is great by itself, but could also make great fajitas!"

INGREDIENTS

1 lime, juiced

1 tablespoon minced garlic

1 teaspoon dried oregano

1 teaspoon ground cumin

2 tablespoons finely chopped canned chipotle peppers in adobo sauce

adobo sauce from canned chipotle peppers to taste

4 (8 ounce) beef sirloin steaks

salt and pepper to taste

DIRECTIONS

1. In a small bowl, mix the lime juice, garlic, oregano, and cumin. Stir in chipotle peppers, and season to taste with adobo sauce.

2. Pierce the meat on both sides with a sharp knife, sprinkle with salt and pepper, and place in a glass dish. Pour lime and chipotle sauce over meat, and turn to coat. Cover, and marinate in the refrigerator for 1 to 2 hours.

3. Preheat grill for high heat.

4. Lightly brush grill grate with oil. Place steaks on the grill, and discard marinade. Grill steaks for 6 minutes per side, or to desired doneness.

China Lake Barbequed Steak

Submitted by: **Bobbie**

Makes: 6 servings

Preparation: 10 minutes

Cooking: 10 minutes

Ready In: 4 hours 20 minutes

"I made this for my family when I was a Navy wife with three children with healthy appetites. This recipe will make the most inexpensive cuts very tender."

INGREDIENTS

1/2 cup soy sauce

1 lemon, juiced

1/4 cup vegetable oil

1/2 tablespoon garlic powder

11/2 pounds flank steak

DIRECTIONS

1. Mix soy sauce, lemon juice and oil together in a large resealable plastic bag. Rub garlic power into meat, place in bag, and seal. Marinate in the refrigerator for at least 4 hours; turn bag after 2 hours.

2. Preheat grill for medium heat.

3. Oil grate lightly, and place meat on grill. Discard marinade. Cook steak for 5 to 7 minutes per side, or to desired doneness.

Flank Steak a la Willyboy

Submitted by: **Willyboyz in the kitchen again**

Makes: 4 servings

Preparation: 15 minutes

Cooking: 15 minutes

Ready In: 24 hours 55 minutes

"You HAVE to let this steak sit overnight. Don't bother making it if you can't put in the time, because the payoff is worth it. This staple in our household is a favorite of all who try it! You can BBQ in summer or broil in the winter for a perfect, filling meal. I like corn on the cob and some sort of rice to complement this mouth watering steak."

INGREDIENTS

1/4 cup honey

1/4 cup soy sauce

1/2 cup red wine

1 clove garlic, crushed

1 pinch dried rosemary, crushed

1 pinch hot chili powder (optional)

1 pinch freshly ground black pepper

1 pound flank steak

DIRECTIONS

1. In a medium bowl, mix together the honey, soy sauce, and red wine. Stir in garlic, rosemary, chili powder, and pepper. Let stand for 15 minutes to blend the flavors.

2. Place the marinade and the steak into a large resealable plastic bag. Press out most of the air, seal, and lay flat in the refrigerator. Refrigerate for 24 hours, turning once halfway through.

3. Preheat grill for high heat.

4. Brush grill grate with oil. Discard marinade, and grill the flank steak for 7 minutes per side, or to desired doneness. Let stand for 10 minutes before slicing very thinly against the grain.

Barbequed Marinated Flank Steak

Makes: 6 servings

Preparation: 15 minutes

Cooking: 10 minutes

Ready In: 8 hours 25 minutes

Submitted by: **Martha Dibblee**

"My butcher Harry at the Eastmoreland Grocery gave me this recipe about 30 years ago. It's easy to make, uses ordinary ingredients, and is delicious barbequed or oven broiled."

INGREDIENTS

1/4 cup soy sauce

3 tablespoons honey

2 tablespoons distilled white vinegar

1/2 teaspoon ground ginger

1/2 teaspoon garlic powder

1/2 cup vegetable oil

1 1/2 pounds flank steak

DIRECTIONS

1. In a blender, combine the soy sauce, honey, vinegar, ginger, garlic powder, and vegetable oil.

2. Lay steak in a shallow glass or ceramic dish. Pierce both sides of the steak with a sharp fork. Pour marinade over steak, then turn and coat the other side. Cover, and refrigerate 8 hours, or overnight.

3. Preheat grill for high heat.

4. Place grate on highest level, and brush lightly with oil. Place steaks on the grill, and discard marinade. Grill steak for 10 minutes, turning once, or to desired doneness.

Marinated Flank Steak

Submitted by: **Connie DiPianta**

Makes: 6 servings

Preparation: 15 minutes

Cooking: 10 minutes

Ready In: 6 hours 25 minutes

"A wonderful flank steak on the grill recipe I invented that friends just love! My girls think this is great, and it doesn't take long to grill. This also works great when sliced and used for fajitas."

INGREDIENTS

1/2 cup vegetable oil

1/3 cup soy sauce

1/4 cup red wine vinegar

2 tablespoons fresh lemon juice

1 1/2 tablespoons Worcestershire sauce

1 tablespoon Dijon mustard

2 cloves garlic, minced

1/2 teaspoon ground black pepper

1 1/2 pounds flank steak

DIRECTIONS

1. In a medium bowl, mix the oil, soy sauce, vinegar, lemon juice, Worcestershire sauce, mustard, garlic, and ground black pepper. Place meat in a shallow glass dish. Pour marinade over the steak, turning meat to coat thoroughly. Cover, and refrigerate for 6 hours.

2. Preheat grill for medium-high heat.

3. Oil the grill grate. Place steaks on the grill, and discard the marinade. Grill meat for 5 minutes per side, or to desired doneness.

Soy Garlic Steak

Submitted by: **Grace**

Makes: 6 servings

Preparation: 15 minutes

Cooking: 10 minutes

Ready In: 3 hours 25 minutes

"A soy sauce and garlic mixture makes for one tasty flank steak marinade."

INGREDIENTS

¼ cup vegetable oil

¼ cup soy sauce

2 tablespoons distilled white vinegar

2 tablespoons ketchup

2 tablespoons crushed garlic

1½ pounds flank steak

DIRECTIONS

1. In a small bowl, mix vegetable oil, soy sauce, vinegar, ketchup, and crushed garlic. Place flank steak in a large resealable plastic bag. Pour the marinade over steak. Seal, and marinate in the refrigerator at least 3 hours.

2. Preheat grill for high heat.

3. Oil the grill grate. Place steaks on the grill, and discard marinade. Cook for 5 minutes per side, or to desired doneness.

London Broil I

Submitted by: **Char Finamore**

Makes: 6 servings

Preparation: 15 minutes

Cooking: 15 minutes

Ready In: 8 hours 30 minutes

"'London broil' most often refers to a thick flank steak, broiled and thinly sliced, but can also refer to thick cuts of sirloin or top round."

INGREDIENTS

3 cloves garlic, minced

1/2 cup soy sauce

2 tablespoons vegetable oil

2 tablespoons ketchup

1 teaspoon dried oregano

1 teaspoon ground black pepper

1 (2 pound) flank steak or round steak

DIRECTIONS

1. In a small bowl, mix together garlic, soy sauce, oil, ketchup, oregano, and black pepper. Pierce meat with a fork on both sides. Place meat and marinade in a large resealable plastic bag. Refrigerate 8 hours, or overnight.

2. Preheat grill for medium-high heat.

3. Lightly oil the grill grate. Place steak on the grill, and discard marinade. Cook for 5 to 8 minutes per side, depending on thickness. Do not overcook, as it is better on the rare side.

Asian Barbequed Steak

Submitted by: **Lesley**

Makes: 8 servings

Preparation: 15 minutes

Cooking: 10 minutes

Ready In: 3 hours 25 minutes

"Thai flavors combine to make one phenomenal steak! Flank steak is our favorite, but it's also great for other cuts of meat. It's great with grilled veggies, and perfect for salads and sandwiches."

INGREDIENTS

1/4 cup chili sauce

1/4 cup fish sauce

1 1/2 tablespoons dark sesame oil

1 tablespoon grated fresh ginger root

3 cloves garlic, peeled and crushed

2 pounds flank steak

DIRECTIONS

1. In a medium bowl, whisk together chili sauce, fish sauce, sesame oil, ginger, and garlic. Set aside a few tablespoons of the mixture for brushing the steaks during grilling. Score flank steak and place in a shallow dish. Pour remaining marinade over the steak, and turn to coat. Cover, and marinate in the refrigerator at least 3 hours.

2. Preheat an outdoor grill for high heat.

3. Lightly brush the grilling surface with oil. Grill steak 5 minutes per side, or to desired doneness, brushing frequently with the reserved marinade mixture.

Bo Nuong Xa

Submitted by: **Maryellen**

Makes: 6 servings

Preparation: 20 minutes

Cooking: 10 minutes

Ready In: 4 hours 30 minutes

"Marinated lemon grass beef skewers that can be broiled or grilled. This is a traditional Vietnamese dish, best if dipped in Nuaoc Cham sauce."

INGREDIENTS

2 teaspoons white sugar

2 tablespoons soy sauce

1 teaspoon ground black pepper

2 cloves garlic, minced

2 stalks lemon grass, minced

2 teaspoons sesame seeds

1½ pounds sirloin tip, thinly sliced

skewers

12 leaves romaine lettuce

fresh cilantro for garnish

fresh basil for garnish

fresh mint for garnish

thinly sliced green onion for garnish

DIRECTIONS

1. In a medium bowl, mix the sugar, soy sauce, pepper, garlic, lemon grass, and sesame seeds. Place the meat in the dish, and stir to coat. Cover, and refrigerate for 4 hours.

2. Preheat grill for high heat. Discard marinade, and thread meat onto skewers accordion style.

3. Brush grill grate with oil, and discard marinade. Arrange skewers on the grill. Cook 5 minutes per side. Serve hot from skewers, or remove from skewers and serve on lettuce leaves. Garnish with cilantro, mint, basil, and sliced green onions.

Kabobs

Submitted by: **Sue**

Makes: 10 servings

Preparation: 30 minutes

Cooking: 10 minutes

Ready In: 4 hours 40 minutes

"Grilled steak and chicken that doesn't dry out on the grill, but stays moist and flavorful. These kabobs are simple to make, and delicious to eat. Skewered meat with peppers, onions, and mushrooms in a honey teriyaki sauce."

INGREDIENTS

1/2 cup teriyaki sauce

1/2 cup honey

1/2 teaspoon garlic powder

1/2 pinch ground ginger

2 red bell peppers, cut into 2 inch pieces

1 large sweet onion, peeled and cut into wedges

1 1/2 cups whole fresh mushrooms

1 pound beef sirloin, cut into 1 inch cubes

1 1/2 pounds skinless, boneless chicken breast halves - cut into cubes

skewers

DIRECTIONS

1. In a large resealable plastic bag, mix the teriyaki sauce, honey, garlic powder, and ginger. Place red bell peppers, onion wedges, mushrooms, beef, and chicken in the bag with the marinade. Seal, and refrigerate 4 to 24 hours.

2. Preheat grill for medium-high heat.

3. Discard marinade, and thread the meat and vegetables onto skewers, leaving a small space between each item.

4. Lightly oil the grill grate. Grill skewers for 10 minutes, turning as needed, or until meat is cooked through and vegetables are tender.

Sensational Sirloin Kabobs

Submitted by: **Kimber**

Makes: 8 servings

Preparation: 15 minutes

Cooking: 15 minutes

Ready In: 8 hours 30 minutes

"After a wild night marinating in a slightly sweet soy sauce and lemon-lime mixture, sirloin steak chunks are skewered with veggies and grilled. You'll want to make these again and again!"

INGREDIENTS

1/4 cup soy sauce

3 tablespoons light brown sugar

3 tablespoons distilled white vinegar

1/2 teaspoon garlic powder

1/2 teaspoon seasoned salt

1/2 teaspoon garlic pepper seasoning

4 fluid ounces lemon-lime flavored carbonated beverage

2 pounds beef sirloin steak, cut into 1 1/2 inch cubes

2 green bell peppers, cut into 2 inch pieces

skewers

1/2 pound fresh mushrooms, stems removed

1 pint cherry tomatoes

1 fresh pineapple - peeled, cored and cubed

DIRECTIONS

1. In a medium bowl, mix soy sauce, light brown sugar, distilled white vinegar, garlic powder, seasoned salt, garlic pepper seasoning, and lemon-lime flavored carbonated beverage. Reserve about ½ cup of this marinade for basting. Place steak in a large resealable plastic bag. Cover with the remaining marinade, and seal. Refrigerate for 8 hours, or overnight.

2. Bring a saucepan of water to a boil. Add green peppers, and cook for 1 minute, just to blanch. Drain, and set aside.

3. Preheat grill for high heat. Thread steak, green peppers, mushrooms, tomatoes, and pineapple onto skewers in an alternating fashion. Discard marinade and the bag.

4. Lightly oil the grill grate. Cook kabobs on the prepared grill for 10 minutes, or to desired doneness. Baste frequently with reserved marinade during the last 5 minutes of cooking.

Best Ever Saucy Beef Kabobs

Submitted by: **Debbie Taber**

Makes: 8 servings

Preparation: 15 minutes

Cooking: 40 minutes

Ready In: 55 minutes

"This is a four star recipe that combines the great taste of grilled beef kabobs with a delicious tomato sauce baste. I always double the sauce to top the beef and veggies over rice. A mouth-watering meal."

INGREDIENTS

2 cups tomato juice

1/2 cup butter

1/4 cup finely chopped onion

1/3 cup ketchup

1 teaspoon dry mustard

1 teaspoon salt

1/2 teaspoon paprika

1/2 teaspoon ground black pepper

1 clove garlic, minced

1 tablespoon Worcestershire sauce

1 dash hot sauce

2 pounds beef sirloin, cut into 1 inch cubes

1/2 pound fresh mushrooms, stems removed

1 pint cherry tomatoes

1 large onion, quartered

1 large green bell pepper, cut into 1 inch pieces

skewers

DIRECTIONS

1. In a saucepan over low heat, mix the tomato juice, butter, onion, ketchup, mustard, salt, paprika, pepper, garlic, Worcestershire sauce, and hot sauce. Simmer for 30 minutes, remove from heat, and allow to cool.

2. Preheat grill for medium heat.

3. Thread the sirloin cubes, mushrooms, cherry tomatoes, onion quarters, and green pepper pieces onto skewers, alternating as desired. Drizzle some of the sauce over the kabobs.

4. Oil the grill grate. Arrange kabobs on the grill. Grill 10 minutes, or until meat is cooked through, occasionally turning kabobs. Baste with sauce during the last 5 minutes.

Asian Beef Skewers

Submitted by: **Vivian Chu**

Makes: 6 servings

Preparation: 30 minutes

Cooking: 6 minutes

Ready In: 2 hours 40 minutes

"Ginger flavored beef skewers are excellent as an appetizer as well as an entree."

INGREDIENTS

3 tablespoons hoisin sauce

3 tablespoons sherry

1/4 cup soy sauce

1 teaspoon barbeque sauce

2 green onions, chopped

2 cloves garlic, minced

1 tablespoon minced fresh ginger root

1 1/2 pounds flank steak

skewers

DIRECTIONS

1. In a small bowl, mix together hoisin sauce, sherry, soy sauce, barbeque sauce, green onions, garlic, and ginger.

2. Cut flank steak across grain on a diagonal into 1/4 inch slices. Place slices in a 1 gallon resealable plastic bag. Pour hoisin sauce mixture over slices, and mix well. Refrigerate 2 hours, or overnight.

3. Preheat an outdoor grill for high heat. Discard marinade, and thread steak on skewers.

4. Oil the grill grate. Grill skewers 3 minutes per side, or to desired doneness.

Blue Cheese Burgers

Submitted by: **Poni**

Makes: 12 servings

Preparation: 15 minutes

Cooking: 10 minutes

Ready In: 2 hours 25 minutes

"Hamburgers? Yes. But basic fare? Definitely not! What a treat they are, and the wise cook will make up a dozen or so for the freezer. If you like blue cheese, you'll never forget these burgers."

INGREDIENTS

3 pounds lean ground beef

4 ounces blue cheese, crumbled

1/2 cup minced fresh chives

1/4 teaspoon hot pepper sauce

1 teaspoon Worcestershire sauce

1 teaspoon coarsely ground black pepper

1 1/2 teaspoons salt

1 teaspoon dry mustard

12 French rolls or hamburger buns

DIRECTIONS

1. In a large bowl, mix the ground beef, blue cheese, chives, hot pepper sauce, Worcestershire sauce, black pepper, salt, and mustard. Cover, and refrigerate for 2 hours.

2. Preheat grill for high heat. Gently form the burger mixture into about 12 patties.

3. Oil the grill grate. Grill patties 5 minutes per side, or until well done. Serve on rolls.

Jalapeno-Garlic-Onion Cheeseburgers

Submitted by: **Steve Hamilton**

Makes: 4 servings

Preparation: 15 minutes

Cooking: 10 minutes

Ready In: 25 minutes

"The three best foods in the world combined in a juicy grilled cheeseburger! These go great with Cowboy Mashed Potatoes!"

INGREDIENTS

1 fresh jalapeno chile pepper, finely chopped

2 cloves garlic, minced

1 small onion, finely chopped

1 pound lean ground beef

4 slices pepperjack cheese

4 hamburger buns

DIRECTIONS

1. Preheat grill for high heat.

2. Mix jalapeno pepper, garlic, onion, and ground beef in a medium bowl. Form into four patties.

3. Brush grill grate with oil. Grill hamburger patties 5 minutes per side, or until well done. Top with pepperjack cheese, and serve on buns.

Spicy Burgers

Submitted by: **Tom**

Makes: 8 servings

Preparation: 15 minutes

Cooking: 10 minutes

Ready In: 25 minutes

"These burgers are chock full of spicy peppers. When handling the chile peppers be sure to wear gloves, and don't let the pepper oils come in contact with your eyes. Serve on buns with your favorite toppings."

INGREDIENTS

2 pounds ground beef

2 teaspoons minced garlic

2 fresh jalapeno peppers, seeded and minced

1 small fresh poblano chile pepper, seeded and minced

1 fresh habanero pepper, seeded and minced (optional)

1 teaspoon crushed red pepper flakes

2 tablespoons chopped fresh cilantro

1 teaspoon ground cumin

DIRECTIONS

1. Preheat grill for high heat.

2. In a large bowl, mix together the beef, garlic, jalapeno peppers, poblano pepper, habanero pepper, red pepper flakes, cilantro, and cumin. Form into burger patties.

3. Lightly oil the grill grate. Place burgers on grill, and cook for 5 minutes per side, or until well done.

Firecracker Burgers

Submitted by: **Gail**

Makes: 4 servings

Preparation: 15 minutes

Cooking: 10 minutes

Ready In: 25 minutes

"This is a great, easy burger recipe. The ground beef is combined with green chile peppers and beef bouillon. This makes them very moist and flavorful. Serve on hamburger buns with your favorite fixings."

INGREDIENTS

1 pound ground beef

1 (4 ounce) can diced green chilies, drained

1 teaspoon beef bouillon granules

4 slices Monterey Jack cheese

DIRECTIONS

1. Preheat grill for high heat.

2. In a medium bowl, mix the beef, diced green chilies, and bouillon. Shape into 4 patties.

3. Lightly oil the grill grate. Grill patties 5 minutes per side, or until well done. Top each patty with cheese about 2 minutes prior to removing from grill.

Cajun Style Burgers

Submitted by: **Gail**

Makes: 4 servings

Preparation: 10 minutes

Cooking: 20 minutes

Ready In: 30 minutes

"These are spicy burgers cooked on the grill and topped with a hot barbeque sauce. Serve with hamburger rolls, lettuce, tomato, and red onion."

INGREDIENTS

1 pound ground beef

3 tablespoons dry bread crumbs

1 egg

3 green onions, chopped

1 tablespoon Cajun seasoning

1 tablespoon prepared mustard

1/4 cup barbeque sauce

1 teaspoon Cajun seasoning

4 slices Cheddar cheese

DIRECTIONS

1. Preheat grill for high heat.

2. In a medium bowl, mix the ground beef, bread crumbs, egg, green onions, 1 tablespoon Cajun seasoning, and mustard. Form into 4 patties.

3. In a small bowl, blend the barbeque sauce and 1 teaspoon Cajun seasoning.

4. Lightly oil the grill grate, and cook the patties 5 minutes per side, or until well done. Place a slice of cheese on each burger, and allow to melt. Serve with seasoned barbeque sauce.

Greek Souzoukaklia

Submitted by: **Marlies Monika**

Makes: 6 servings

Preparation: 30 minutes

Cooking: 15 minutes

Ready In: 45 minutes

"An extraordinary barbecue recipe to surprise friends and family. Serve with lemon slices and rice."

INGREDIENTS

1¹/₂ pounds ground beef

1 onion, chopped

³/₈ cup raisins, chopped

1¹/₂ teaspoons chopped flat leaf parsley

¹/₂ teaspoon cayenne pepper

¹/₂ teaspoon ground cinnamon

¹/₂ teaspoon ground coriander

1 pinch ground nutmeg

¹/₂ teaspoon white sugar

salt and pepper to taste

skewers

1 tablespoon vegetable oil

DIRECTIONS

1. Preheat grill for high heat.

2. In a large bowl, mix together ground beef, onion, raisins, and parsley. Season with cayenne pepper, cinnamon, coriander, nutmeg, sugar, salt, and pepper, and mix well. Form into 6 flat sausages around skewers. Lightly brush sausages with oil; this prevents sticking to the grill.

3. Arrange skewers on hot grill grate. Cook for approximately 15 minutes, turning occasionally to brown evenly, until well done.

Juiciest Hamburgers Ever

Submitted by: **Jane**

Makes: 8 servings

Preparation: 15 minutes

Cooking: 10 minutes

Ready In: 35 minutes

"No more dry, lackluster burgers. These are juicy, and spices can be easily added or changed to suit anyone's taste. Baste frequently with your favorite barbeque sauce. If you find the meat mixture too mushy, just add more bread crumbs until it forms patties that hold their shape."

INGREDIENTS

2 pounds ground beef

1 egg, beaten

3/4 cup dry bread crumbs

3 tablespoons evaporated milk

2 tablespoons Worcestershire sauce

1/8 teaspoon cayenne pepper

2 cloves garlic, minced

DIRECTIONS

1. Preheat grill for high heat.

2. In a large bowl, mix the ground beef, egg, bread crumbs, evaporated milk, Worcestershire sauce, cayenne pepper, and garlic using your hands. Form the mixture into 8 hamburger patties.

3. Lightly oil the grill grate. Grill patties 5 minutes per side, or until well done.

Game Day Hamburgers

Submitted by: **Andy Alcorn**

Makes: 6 servings

Preparation: 20 minutes

Cooking: 10 minutes

Ready In: 30 minutes

"These are seasoned and stuffed hamburgers with a taste of potato and cheese. Serve on buns with condiments of choice."

INGREDIENTS

1 large potato, peeled and shredded

1 cup shredded Swiss cheese

1 cup chopped fresh mushrooms

2 pounds lean ground beef

2 (1 ounce) packages dry onion soup mix

DIRECTIONS

1. Preheat grill for high heat.

2. In a medium bowl, mix together potato, cheese, and mushrooms.

3. In a large bowl, mix ground beef with onion soup mix. Form into 6 large burger patties. Make a pocket in each burger, stuff with potato mixture, and seal.

4. When ready to grill, brush grate with oil. Cook burgers over high heat for 5 minutes on each side, or until well done. Serve hot.

Hobo's Delight

Submitted by: **Michelle**

Makes: 6 servings

Preparation: 15 minutes

Cooking: 30 minutes

Ready In: 45 minutes

"This recipe combines hamburgers with onions, baby carrots, and potatoes in individually cooked foil packets. This makes clean up a snap, and keeps the grill clean, too. This also works well with round steaks."

INGREDIENTS

2 pounds lean ground beef

1 onion, sliced

1 (16 ounce) package baby carrots

4 potatoes, peeled and sliced

seasoned salt to taste

salt and black pepper to taste

DIRECTIONS

1. Preheat grill for medium-high heat.

2. Form the ground beef into individual patties, and place each patty on a piece of foil large enough to hold the patty and some vegetables. Layer each patty with onion slices, carrots, and potato slices. Season with seasoned salt, salt, and pepper to taste. Wrap foil around food, and seal each packet tightly.

3. Grill 30 minutes, or until the potatoes are tender. Carefully open each packet (the steam that escapes will be very hot), and serve.

Asian Barbequed Butterflied Leg of Lamb

Submitted by: **Cyndi**

Makes: 10 servings
Preparation: 15 minutes
Cooking: 30 minutes
Ready In: 9 hours

"Inspired by Mongolian Beef and the Korean short ribs my grandfather always made for special occasions. Have your butcher trim, split, and debone a whole leg of lamb for you. Make the marinade (also good on ribs, or steak, or pork). Marinate overnight. Grill the meat to desired doneness. Slice to serve. We like it wrapped in tortillas or flatbreads with leaves of butter lettuce."

INGREDIENTS

2/3 cup hoisin sauce

6 tablespoons rice vinegar

1/2 cup minced green onions

1/4 cup mushroom soy sauce

4 tablespoons minced garlic

2 tablespoons honey

1/2 teaspoon sesame oil

1 tablespoon toasted sesame seeds

1/2 teaspoon ground white pepper

1/2 teaspoon freshly ground black pepper

1 (5 pound) boneless butterflied leg of lamb

DIRECTIONS

1. In a large resealable plastic bag, mix hoisin sauce, rice vinegar, green onions, mushroom soy sauce, garlic, honey, sesame oil, sesame seeds, white pepper, and black pepper. Place lamb in bag, seal, and turn to coat. Refrigerate for 8 hours, or overnight.

2. Preheat grill for high heat.

3. Oil the grill grate. Place lamb on the grill, and discard marinade. Cook 15 minutes on each side, to a minimum internal temperature of 145°F (63°C), or to desired doneness. Transfer meat to a serving platter, and allow it to rest for 20 minutes before slicing and serving.

Grilled Lamb with Brown Sugar Glaze

Submitted by: **Deborah Bonzey**

Makes: 4 servings

Preparation: 15 minutes

Cooking: 10 minutes

Ready In: 1 hour 25 minutes

"Sweet and savory, perfect for a spring meal with noodles and a green vegetable. Chops need to marinate one hour."

INGREDIENTS

1/4 cup brown sugar

2 teaspoons ground ginger

2 teaspoons dried tarragon

1 teaspoon ground cinnamon

1 teaspoon ground black pepper

1 teaspoon garlic powder

1/2 teaspoon salt

4 lamb chops

DIRECTIONS

1. In a medium bowl, mix brown sugar, ginger, tarragon, cinnamon, pepper, garlic powder, and salt. Rub lamb chops with the seasonings, and place on a plate. Cover, and refrigerate for 1 hour.

2. Preheat grill for high heat.

3. Brush grill grate lightly with oil, and arrange lamb chops on grill. Cook 5 minutes on each side, or to desired doneness.

Lemon and Thyme Lamb Chops

Submitted by: **Diane**

Makes: 12 servings

Preparation: 10 minutes

Cooking: 10 minutes

Ready In: 1 hour 20 minutes

"Drag that grill out of storage for spring grilling! Make extra marinade to use on grilled vegetables. Serve with a mint sauce and warmed flatbread."

INGREDIENTS

1/2 cup olive oil

1/4 cup lemon juice

1 tablespoon chopped fresh thyme

salt and pepper to taste

12 lamb chops

DIRECTIONS

1. Stir together olive oil, lemon juice, and thyme in a small bowl. Season with salt and pepper to taste. Place lamb chops in a shallow dish, and brush with the olive oil mixture. Marinate in the refrigerator for 1 hour.

2. Preheat grill for high heat.

3. Lightly oil grill grate. Place lamb chops on grill, and discard marinade. Cook for 10 minutes, turning once, or to desired doneness.

Indian Style Sheekh Kabab

Submitted by: **Yakuta**

Makes: 8 servings

Preparation: 15 minutes

Cooking: 10 minutes

Ready In: 2 hours 25 minutes

"This is a spicy and extremely flavorful recipe which will surely be a hit at any BBQ party."

INGREDIENTS

2 pounds lean ground lamb

2 onions, finely chopped

1/2 cup fresh mint leaves, finely chopped

1/2 cup cilantro, finely chopped

1 tablespoon ginger paste

1 tablespoon green chile paste

2 teaspoons ground cumin

2 teaspoons ground coriander

2 teaspoons paprika

1 teaspoon cayenne pepper

2 teaspoons salt

1/4 cup vegetable oil

skewers

DIRECTIONS

1. In a large bowl, mix ground lamb, onions, mint, cilantro, ginger paste, and chile paste. Season with cumin, coriander, paprika, cayenne, and salt. Cover, and refrigerate for 2 hours.

2. Mold handfuls of the lamb mixture, about 1 cup, to form sausages around skewers. Make sure the meat is spread to an even thickness. Refrigerate until you are ready to grill.

3. Preheat grill for high heat.

4. Brush grate liberally with oil, and arrange kabobs on grill. Cook for 10 minutes, or until well done, turning as needed to brown evenly.

Grilled Spicy Lamb Burgers

Submitted by: **Alan Hollister**

Makes: 4 servings

Preparation: 15 minutes

Cooking: 10 minutes

Ready In: 25 minutes

"Something new for all the grill-daddies! An EASY burger to make, and guests rave over this one."

INGREDIENTS

1 pound ground lamb

2 tablespoons chopped fresh mint leaves

2 tablespoons chopped fresh cilantro

2 tablespoons chopped fresh oregano

1 tablespoon garlic, chopped

1 teaspoon sherry

1 teaspoon white wine vinegar

1 teaspoon molasses

1 teaspoon ground cumin

1/4 teaspoon ground allspice

1/2 teaspoon red pepper flakes

1/2 teaspoon salt

1/2 teaspoon ground black pepper

4 pita bread rounds

4 ounces feta cheese, crumbled

DIRECTIONS

1. Preheat grill for medium heat.

2. Place the lamb in a large bowl, and mix with the mint, cilantro, oregano, garlic, sherry, vinegar, and molasses. Season with cumin, allspice, red pepper flakes, salt, and black pepper, and mix well. Shape into 4 patties.

3. Brush grill grate with oil. Grill burgers 5 minutes on each side, or until well done. Heat the pita pocket briefly on the grill. Serve burgers wrapped in pitas with feta cheese.

pork

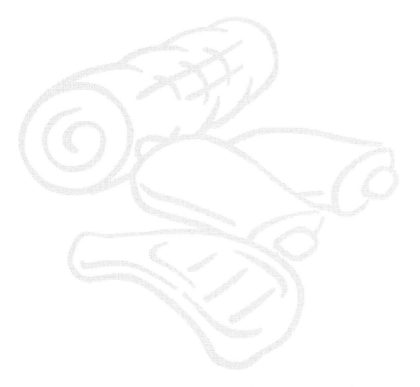

Once you taste tender shreds of pulled pork piled high on a bun, or sticky, spice-doused ribs so irresistible that you can't help gnawing 'til the last shred is long gone, you'll know why, in some parts of the world, pork is the very definition of barbeque. And no matter where you are, chops, loin, and sausage alike are improved by a trip over the flames.

Honey Mustard BBQ Pork Chops

Makes: 8 servings

Preparation: 15 minutes

Cooking: 15 minutes

Ready In: 2 hours 30 minutes

Submitted by: **Jody Champion**

"These pork chops are great! I accidentally left them in the marinade for a day, a night, and the next day, and they were even better! They are very tender and tasty."

INGREDIENTS

1/3 cup honey

3 tablespoons orange juice

1 tablespoon apple cider vinegar

1 teaspoon white wine

1 teaspoon Worcestershire sauce

2 teaspoons onion powder, or to taste

1/4 teaspoon dried tarragon

3 tablespoons Dijon mustard

8 thin cut pork chops

DIRECTIONS

1. Place honey, orange juice, vinegar, wine, Worcestershire sauce, onion powder, tarragon, and mustard in a large resealable plastic bag. Slash fatty edge of each chop in about three places without cutting into the meat; this will prevent the meat from curling during cooking. Place chops in the plastic bag, and marinate in the refrigerator for at least 2 hours.

2. Preheat grill for high heat.

3. Lightly oil grill grate. Place chops on grill, and discard marinade. Cook chops for 6 to 8 minutes, turning once, or to desired doneness.

Mesquite Grilled Pork Chops with Apple Salsa

Submitted by: **Wendy Furbay**

Makes: 4 servings

Preparation: 20 minutes

Cooking: 8 minutes

Ready In: 3 hours 28 minutes

"The Southwestern version of 'pork chops and apple-sauce.' They'll want the recipe!"

INGREDIENTS

1 (16 ounce) jar applesauce

1 onion, quartered

1 jalapeno pepper, seeded and minced

1 clove garlic, minced

½ teaspoon salt

1 tablespoon ground white pepper

4 pork chops

1½ teaspoons garlic powder

salt and pepper to taste

1 cup mesquite chips, soaked

DIRECTIONS

1. In a medium bowl, combine applesauce, onion, jalapeno pepper, garlic, ½ teaspoon salt, and white pepper. Refrigerate several hours, or overnight.

2. Season chops with garlic powder, and salt and pepper to taste.

3. Preheat grill for medium-high heat.

4. Sprinkle soaked wood over coals, or place in the smoker box of a gas grill. Lightly oil grate, and place chops on grill. Cook for 6 to 8 minutes per side, or to desired doneness. Serve with applesauce salsa.

Tasty Orange Chops

Submitted by: **Diana Rios**

Makes: 4 servings

Preparation: 15 minutes

Cooking: 8 minutes

Ready In: 6 hours 23 minutes

"Try this recipe at least once. You really will like it. This is one of the few ways my family will eat pork, and they love it."

INGREDIENTS

1/4 cup cider vinegar

1 tablespoon soy sauce

1/2 cup frozen orange juice concentrate, thawed

1/2 onion, shredded

1 teaspoon dried rosemary

1 teaspoon ground sage

2 teaspoons salt, or to taste

1 large clove garlic, crushed

1/2 cup barbeque sauce

4 thick cut pork chops

DIRECTIONS

1. In a mixing bowl, mix together vinegar, soy sauce, orange juice, onion, rosemary, sage, salt, garlic, and barbecue sauce. Place chops in a large resealable plastic bag. Pour in the marinade, and seal. Refrigerate for 6 to 8 hours, or overnight.

2. Preheat grill for high heat. Transfer marinade to a small saucepan, bring to a boil, and cook for several minutes.

3. Lightly oil preheated grill. Grill chops for 6 to 8 minutes, turning once, or to desired doneness. Brush cooked marinade over chops during the final minutes of cooking.

Caribbean Jerk Pork Chops

Submitted by: **Marvin**

Makes: 6 servings
Preparation: 15 minutes
Cooking: 10 minutes
Ready In: 12 hours 30 minutes

"Caribbean-style pork chops marinated overnight in a lemon juice and oil marinade with a variety of spices. Use more cayenne pepper to make it really hot!"

INGREDIENTS

3/4 cup water

1/3 cup lemon juice

1/3 cup chopped onion

1 tablespoon packed brown sugar

1 tablespoon chopped green onion

1 tablespoon canola oil

3/4 teaspoon salt

3/4 teaspoon ground allspice

3/4 teaspoon ground cinnamon

3/4 teaspoon ground black pepper

1/2 teaspoon dried thyme, crushed

1/4 teaspoon cayenne pepper, or to taste

6 lean pork chops, 1/2 inch thick

DIRECTIONS

1. Combine water, lemon juice, onion, brown sugar, green onions, oil, salt, allspice, cinnamon, black pepper, thyme, and cayenne pepper in a blender or food processor. Blend until smooth. Reserve ½ cup for basting.

2. Place pork chops in shallow glass dish. Pour remaining marinade over the meat. Cover, and refrigerate at least 12 hours, but no longer than 24 hours.

3. Preheat grill for medium heat. Place grate 4 to 5 inches above heat source.

4. Oil the grill grate. Arrange chops on grate, and discard marinade. Cover grill, and cook chops for 10 minutes, turning once, or to desired doneness.

Tangy Grilled Pork Tenderloin

Submitted by: **Colleen**

Makes: 6 servings

Preparation: 15 minutes

Cooking: 25 minutes

Ready In: 4 hours 40 minutes

"This is a quick, easy and very flavorful recipe. I've made it many times. Plan ahead because the pork needs to marinate."

INGREDIENTS

2 pounds pork tenderloin

2/3 cup honey

1/2 cup Dijon mustard

1/4 teaspoon chili powder

1/4 teaspoon salt

DIRECTIONS

1. Place meat in a large resealable plastic bag. In a medium bowl, mix together honey, Dijon mustard, chili powder, and salt. Pour marinade over tenderloins, seal, and refrigerate for at least 4 hours.

2. Prepare the grill for indirect heat.

3. Lightly oil grill grate. Remove meat from marinade, and discard liquid. Grill for 15 to 25 minutes, or to desired doneness.

Grecian Pork Tenderloin

Submitted by: **Dave Nash**

Makes: 6 servings

Preparation: 15 minutes

Cooking: 30 minutes

Ready In: 2 hours 45 minutes

"Lean and tender, pork tenderloins are perfect for the grill. This zesty marinade makes tenderloins even more tender than they already are."

INGREDIENTS

1½ cups fresh lime juice

¾ cup olive oil

6 cloves garlic, sliced

2 teaspoons salt

6 tablespoons dried oregano

2 (1 pound) pork tenderloins

DIRECTIONS

1. Place lime juice, olive oil, garlic, salt, and oregano in a large resealable plastic bag. Shake sealed bag until ingredients are well mixed. Taste the marinade for tartness. If too tart, add a little more oil. Not enough zing, add more lime. The garlic and salt flavors should also be up front, yet not overpowering. Place tenderloins in the bag, seal, and turn to coat. Marinate in the refrigerator for 2 to 5 hours.

2. Preheat grill for medium heat.

3. Lightly oil the grill grate, and discard marinade. Grill tenderloins for 20 to 30 minutes, turning once, or to desired doneness.

Grilled Pork Tenderloin

Submitted by: **Cathy Christensen**

Makes: 6 servings

Preparation: 10 minutes

Cooking: 45 minutes

Ready In: 55 minutes

"This is one of my family's favorites. This pork recipe is always tender and juicy. Serve with additional barbeque sauce for dipping."

INGREDIENTS

2 (1 pound) pork tenderloins

1 teaspoon garlic powder

1 teaspoon salt

1 teaspoon ground black pepper

1 cup barbeque sauce

DIRECTIONS

1. Prepare grill for indirect heat.

2. Season meat with garlic powder, salt, and pepper.

3. Lightly oil grate. Place tenderloin on grate, and position drip pan under meat. Cook over indirect heat for 30 minutes.

4. Brush tenderloin with barbeque sauce. Continue cooking for 15 minutes, or to desired doneness. Slice pork, and serve.

Marinated Pork Tenderloin

Submitted by: **Lisa**

Makes: 4 servings

Preparation: 10 minutes

Cooking: 20 minutes

Ready In: 6 hours 30 minutes

"A slightly sweet marinade that makes for the best tasting pork you will ever have."

INGREDIENTS

1/4 cup soy sauce

1/4 cup packed brown sugar

2 tablespoons sherry

1 1/2 teaspoons dried minced onion

1 teaspoon ground cinnamon

2 tablespoons olive oil

1 pinch garlic powder

2 (3/4 pound) pork tenderloins

DIRECTIONS

1. Place soy sauce, brown sugar, sherry, dried onion, cinnamon, olive oil, and a touch of garlic powder in a large resealable plastic bag. Seal, and shake to mix. Place pork in bag with marinade, seal, and refrigerate for 6 to 12 hours.

2. Preheat grill for high heat.

3. Lightly oil grate. Place tenderloins on grill, and discard marinade. Cook 20 minutes, or to desired doneness. Slice into medallions, and serve.

Fruity Grilled Pork Tenderloin

Submitted by: **Kris Schultz**

Makes: 2 servings

Preparation: 15 minutes

Cooking: 30 minutes

Ready In: 4 hours 45 minutes

"This is my favorite summer marinade for pork tender-loin. Use any of your favorite fruit sodas - black cherry, grape, raspberry, etc. Also great served cold on a green salad."

INGREDIENTS

1/4 cup soy sauce

1/3 cup packed brown sugar

1/3 cup plum jam

3/4 cup black cherry soda

1 (1 pound) pork tenderloin

DIRECTIONS

1. In a small sauce pan, mix together soy sauce, brown sugar, and jam over low heat until sugar has dissolved. Reserve 1/4 cup of sauce for basting the tenderloin while grilling. Combine remaining sauce with soda in a large plastic resealable bag; place meat in bag, and seal. Marinate in the refrigerator for at least 4 hours, or overnight.

2. Preheat grill for medium heat.

3. Lightly oil preheated grill, and discard marinade. Cook tenderloin for 15 to 20 minutes, or to desired doneness, basting occasionally with reserved sauce. Remove meat from grill, and allow to rest for 5 minutes before slicing into 1/4 inch thick medallions.

Pork Tenderloin with a Honey Grape Sauce

Submitted by: **Linda VanHoose**

Makes: 6 servings

Preparation: 15 minutes

Cooking: 25 minutes

Ready In: 40 minutes

"Grilled pork tenderloin served with a sauce made with shallots, garlic, honey, grapes, and ginger. Simple preparation with an exotic taste."

INGREDIENTS

salt and freshly ground black pepper to taste

2 pounds pork tenderloin

2 teaspoons olive oil

1/4 cup minced shallots

1 tablespoon minced garlic

2 cups seedless red grapes, halved

2 tablespoons soy sauce

2 tablespoons honey

1 teaspoon grated fresh ginger root

1/2 teaspoon Asian five-spice powder

DIRECTIONS

1. Preheat grill for medium heat.

2. Lightly oil grate. Season meat with salt and pepper, and place on grill. Cook for 15 to 25 minutes, or to desired doneness, turning meat as necessary to cook evenly. Remove from grill, and let stand 10 minutes before slicing.

3. Meanwhile, heat olive oil in a saucepan over medium heat. Cook shallots and garlic in oil until tender. Stir in grapes, soy sauce, honey, ginger, and five-spice powder. Bring to a boil. Reduce heat, and simmer for 15 minutes. Set aside to cool for 10 minutes.

4. Process cooled sauce until smooth in a blender or food processor. Serve over sliced tenderloin.

North Carolina-Style Pulled Pork

Submitted by: **Doug**

Makes: 10 servings
Preparation: 1 hour
Cooking: 6 hours
Ready In: 15 hours

"This recipe is delicious, especially when smoked with hickory chips on a charcoal grill. A spicy rub and a zesty vinegar sauce turn pork into a North Carolina favorite."

INGREDIENTS

1 tablespoon mild paprika

2 teaspoons light brown sugar

1 1/2 teaspoons hot paprika

1/2 teaspoon celery salt

1/2 teaspoon garlic salt

1/2 teaspoon dry mustard

1/2 teaspoon ground black pepper

1/2 teaspoon onion powder

1/4 teaspoon salt

8 pounds pork butt roast

2 cups cider vinegar

1 1/3 cups water

5/8 cup ketchup

1/4 cup firmly packed brown sugar

5 teaspoons salt

4 teaspoons crushed red pepper flakes

1 teaspoon ground black pepper

1 teaspoon ground white pepper

2 pounds hickory wood chips, soaked

DIRECTIONS

1. In a small bowl, mix mild paprika, light brown sugar, hot paprika, celery salt, garlic salt, dry mustard, ground black pepper, onion powder, and salt. Rub spice mixture into the roast on all sides. Wrap in plastic wrap, and refrigerate 8 hours, or overnight.

2. Prepare a grill for indirect heat.

3. Sprinkle a handful of soaked wood over coals, or place in the smoker box of a gas grill. Place pork butt roast on the grate over a drip pan. Cover grill, and cook pork at least 6 hours, or until the internal temperature reaches a minimum of 195°F (200°C). Check hourly, adding fresh coals and hickory chips as necessary to maintain heat and smoke.

4. Remove pork from heat and place on a cutting board. Allow the meat to cool approximately 15 minutes, then shred into bite-sized pieces using two forks. This requires patience.

5. In a medium bowl, whisk together cider vinegar, water, ketchup, brown sugar, salt, red pepper flakes, black pepper, and white pepper. Continue whisking until brown sugar and salt have dissolved. Place shredded pork and vinegar sauce in a large roasting pan, and stir to coat pork. Serve immediately, or cover and keep warm on the grill for up to one hour until serving.

Marinated Pork Roast

Submitted by: **Denise Hummel**

Makes: 8 servings

Preparation: 15 minutes

Cooking: 2 hours

Ready In: 4 hours 15 minutes

"This is a great marinade for any meat. I especially like it on pork roasts, but it can easily be used on chicken or ribs."

INGREDIENTS

1 (4 pound) pork roast

1/2 cup Worcestershire sauce

2 tablespoons honey

2 tablespoons cider vinegar

1/2 teaspoon mustard seed

1/2 teaspoon mustard powder

1 teaspoon lemon pepper

1/2 teaspoon celery salt

1 clove garlic, minced

DIRECTIONS

1. Prepare grill for indirect heat.

2. In a large resealable plastic bag, combine the Worcestershire sauce, honey, vinegar, mustard seed, mustard powder, lemon pepper, celery salt, and garlic; seal, and mix ingredients. Place the roast in the plastic bag, press air out of bag, and seal. Marinate for 2 hours in the refrigerator, turning the roast occasionally to help coat while marinating.

3. Lightly oil grill grate. Place roast on grill, and discard marinade. Cover, and cook for 1½ to 2 hours, or until internal temperature is 160°F (70°C).

Barbecue Ribs

Submitted by: **Kristy**

Makes: 8 servings
Preparation: 15 minutes
Cooking: 2 hours
Ready In: 3 hours 15 minutes

"This recipe is easier than it sounds. I usually cook the ribs the day before and grill them for a quick dinner the next night. FYI: the sauce is much better after it is cooked. It is not a dipping sauce."

INGREDIENTS

4 pounds pork spareribs

1 cup brown sugar

1/4 cup ketchup

1/4 cup soy sauce

1/4 cup Worcestershire sauce

1/4 cup rum

1/2 cup chile sauce

2 cloves garlic, crushed

1 teaspoon dry mustard

1 dash ground black pepper

DIRECTIONS

1. Preheat oven to 350°F (175°C). Cut spareribs into serving size portions, wrap in double thickness of foil, and bake for 1½ hours. Unwrap, and drain drippings. (I usually freeze the drippings to use later in soups.) Place ribs in a large roasting pan.

2. In a bowl, mix together brown sugar, ketchup, soy sauce, Worcestershire sauce, rum, chile sauce, garlic, mustard, and pepper. Coat ribs with sauce and marinate at room temperature for 1 hour, or refrigerate overnight.

3. Preheat grill for medium heat. Position grate four inches above heat source.

4. Brush grill grate with oil. Place ribs on grill, and cook for 30 minutes, basting with marinade.

Texas Pork Ribs

Submitted by: **Laura Walton**

Makes: 12 servings

Preparation: 30 minutes

Cooking: 5 hours

Ready In: 13 hours 30 minutes

"This is a multiple prize-winning master recipe. It has several steps that can be used on pork spareribs, country style ribs, or pretty much any other type of pork rib; simply adjust oven time up for meatier cuts. Try to use some smoking chips on the barbecue. The smokier the grill, the better the ribs will taste!"

INGREDIENTS

6 pounds pork spareribs

1 1/2 cups white sugar

1/4 cup salt

2 1/2 tablespoons ground black pepper

3 tablespoons sweet paprika

1 teaspoon cayenne pepper, or to taste

2 tablespoons garlic powder

5 tablespoons pan drippings

1/2 cup chopped onion

4 cups ketchup

3 cups hot water

4 tablespoons brown sugar

cayenne pepper to taste

salt and pepper to taste

1 cup wood chips, soaked

DIRECTIONS

1. Clean the ribs, and trim away any excess fat. In a medium bowl, stir together the sugar, 1/4 cup salt, ground black pepper, paprika, 1 teaspoon cayenne pepper, and garlic powder. Coat ribs liberally with spice mix. Place the ribs in two 10x15 inch roasting pans, piling two racks of ribs per pan. Cover, and refrigerate for at least 8 hours.

2. Preheat oven to 275°F (135°C). Bake uncovered for 3 to 4 hours, or until the ribs are tender and nearly fall apart.

3. Remove 5 tablespoons of drippings from the bottom of the roasting pans, and place in a skillet over medium heat. Cook onion in pan drippings until lightly browned and tender. Stir in ketchup, and heat for 3 to 4 more minutes, stirring constantly. Next, mix in water and brown sugar, and season to taste with cayenne pepper, salt, and pepper. Reduce heat to low, cover, and simmer for 1 hour, adding water as necessary to achieve desired thickness.

4. Preheat grill for medium-low heat.

5. When ready to grill, add soaked wood chips to the coals or to the smoker box of a gas grill. Lightly oil grill grate. Place ribs on the grill two racks at a time so they are not crowded. Cook for 20 minutes, turning occasionally. Baste ribs with sauce during the last 10 minutes of grilling, so the sauce does not burn.

Simple Country Ribs

Submitted by: **Tammi**

Makes: 4 servings

Preparation: 10 minutes

Cooking: 1 hour

Ready In: 1 hour 10 minutes

"Extra tender, extra flavorful ribs, bursting with barbeque flavor."

INGREDIENTS

2½ pounds pork spareribs

2 (18 ounce) bottles barbeque sauce

1 onion, quartered

1 teaspoon salt

½ teaspoon ground black pepper

DIRECTIONS

1. Place spareribs in a large stock pot with barbeque sauce, onion, salt, and pepper. Pour in enough water to cover. Bring to a low boil, and cook approximately 40 minutes.

2. Preheat grill for high heat.

3. Lightly oil grate. Remove spareribs from the stock pot, and place on the prepared grill. Use the barbeque sauce in the saucepan to baste ribs while cooking. Grill ribs, basting and turning frequently, for 20 minutes, or until nicely browned.

Barbequed Pork Ribs

Submitted by: **Robbie Rice**

Makes: 10 servings

Preparation: 20 minutes

Cooking: 1 hour 20 minutes

Ready In: 3 hours 40 minutes

"This is an excellent dish for a barbeque party. Make the ribs in advance, and when your guests have arrived, all that's left to do is the grilling. You'll have them wondering how they got so tender and tasty so fast."

INGREDIENTS

5 pounds pork spareribs, cut into serving size pieces

1/2 cup butter

1 medium onion, chopped

1 tablespoon minced garlic

1/2 cup distilled white vinegar

1 cup water

1 cup ketchup

1 cup hickory smoke flavored barbeque sauce

1 lemon, juiced

salt and pepper to taste

DIRECTIONS

1. Place ribs in large skillet or roasting pan. Cover with lightly salted water, and bring to a boil. Reduce heat to low, and simmer for 1 hour, or until meat is tender, but not quite falling off the bone. Remove from heat, and drain.

2. Place the boiled ribs in a roasting pan, and cover with sauce. Cover, and refrigerate for at least 2 hours.

3. Melt butter in a saucepan over medium heat. Cook the onion and garlic in butter until the onion is tender; remove from heat. In a blender, combine 1 cup water, vinegar, ketchup, barbeque sauce, and lemon juice. Pour in the melted butter mixture, and puree for 1 minute. Pour into a saucepan, and season to taste with salt and pepper. Bring to a boil, then remove from heat.

4. Preheat grill for medium-high heat.

5. Brush grill grate with oil. Grill ribs for 10 to 20 minutes, or until well browned, basting with sauce and turning frequently.

Freak'n Good Ribs

Submitted by: **Mike B. - Orleans, Ontario**

Makes: 4 servings

Preparation: 30 minutes

Cooking: 2 hours

Ready In: 10 hours 30 minutes

"Pineapple-marinated pork back ribs! This recipe doubles easily for more ribs."

INGREDIENTS

3 cups pineapple juice

1 1/2 cups brown sugar

1 1/2 tablespoons mustard powder

1/3 cup ketchup

1/3 cup red wine vinegar

1 1/2 tablespoons fresh lemon juice

2 tablespoons soy sauce

1/2 teaspoon ground cloves

2 teaspoons ground ginger

4 cloves garlic, minced

1/2 teaspoon cayenne pepper

2 pounds baby back pork ribs

1 (18 ounce) bottle barbeque sauce

DIRECTIONS

1. In a large baking dish, mix together the pineapple juice, brown sugar, mustard powder, ketchup, red wine vinegar, lemon juice, and soy sauce. Season with cloves, ginger, garlic, and cayenne pepper. Cut ribs into serving size pieces, and place into the marinade. Cover, and refrigerate, turning occasionally, for 8 hours or overnight.

2. Preheat oven to 275°F (80°C). Cook ribs in marinade for 1½ hours, turning occasionally to ensure even cooking.

3. Preheat grill for medium heat.

4. Lightly oil grate. Grill ribs for 15 to 20 minutes, basting with barbecue sauce, and turning frequently until nicely glazed.

Prize Winning Baby Back Ribs

Submitted by: **Bonnie Quinn**

Makes: 6 servings

Preparation: 20 minutes

Cooking: 1 hour 5 minutes

Ready In: 1 hour 25 minutes

"A foolproof, simple recipe for the most tender, delectable ribs you've ever had. Follow the directions exactly, and success is guaranteed!"

INGREDIENTS

1 tablespoon ground cumin

1 tablespoon chili powder

1 tablespoon paprika

salt and pepper to taste

3 pounds baby back pork ribs

1 cup barbeque sauce

DIRECTIONS

1. Preheat grill for high heat.

2. In a small jar, combine cumin, chili powder, paprika, salt, and pepper. Close the lid, and shake to mix.

3. Trim the membrane sheath from the back of each rack. Run a small, sharp knife between the membrane and each rib, and snip off the membrane as much as possible. Sprinkle as much of the rub onto both sides of the ribs as desired. To prevent the ribs from becoming too dark and spicy, do not thoroughly rub the spices into the ribs. Store the unused portion of the spice mix for future use.

4. Place aluminum foil on lower rack to capture drippings and prevent flare-ups. Lightly oil grate, and lay ribs on top rack of grill. Reduce heat to low, close lid, and leave undisturbed for 1 hour. Do not lift lid at all.

5. Brush ribs with barbecue sauce, and grill an additional 5 minutes. Serve ribs as whole rack, or cut between each rib bone and pile individually on a platter.

Maple Glazed Ribs

Submitted by: **Karen Toellner**

Makes: 6 servings

Preparation: 15 minutes

Cooking: 1 hour 25 minutes

Ready In: 3 hours 40 minutes

"Basted with a savory sweet sauce, these ribs are definitely finger-licking good!"

INGREDIENTS

3 pounds baby back pork ribs

3/4 cup maple syrup

2 tablespoons packed brown sugar

2 tablespoons ketchup

1 tablespoon cider vinegar

1 tablespoon Worcestershire sauce

1/2 teaspoon salt

1/2 teaspoon mustard powder

DIRECTIONS

1. Place ribs in a large pot, and cover with water. Cover, and simmer for 1 hour, or until meat is tender. Drain, and transfer ribs to a shallow dish.

2. In a small saucepan, stir together the maple syrup, brown sugar, ketchup, vinegar, Worcestershire sauce, salt, and mustard powder. Bring to a low boil, and cook for 5 minutes, stirring frequently. Cool slightly, then pour over ribs, and marinate in the refrigerator for 2 hours.

3. Prepare grill for cooking with indirect heat. Remove ribs from marinade. Transfer marinade to a small saucepan, and boil for several minutes.

4. Lightly oil grate. Cook for about 20 minutes, basting with the cooked marinade frequently, until nicely glazed.

Barbequed Ribs

Submitted by: **Gail**

Makes: 8 servings

Preparation: 30 minutes

Cooking: 3 hours

Ready In: 11 hours 30 minutes

"Two day ribs, but worth the effort. Baked and marinated with a rub overnight, then grilled with barbecue sauce."

INGREDIENTS

4 pounds baby back pork ribs

4 cloves garlic, sliced

1 tablespoon white sugar

1 tablespoon paprika

2 teaspoons salt

2 teaspoons ground black pepper

2 teaspoons chili powder

2 teaspoons ground cumin

1/2 cup dark brown sugar

1/2 cup cider vinegar

1/2 cup ketchup

1/4 cup chili sauce

1/4 cup Worcestershire sauce

1 tablespoon lemon juice

2 tablespoons onion, chopped

1/2 teaspoon dry mustard

1 clove crushed garlic

DIRECTIONS

1. Preheat oven to 300°F (150°C). Place ribs on a rack in a shallow roasting pan. Scatter 4 cloves of sliced garlic over ribs. Cover, and bake for 2½ hours. Cool slightly.

2. In a small bowl, mix together white sugar, paprika, salt, black pepper, chili powder, and ground cumin. Rub spices over cooled ribs. Cover, and refrigerate overnight.

3. In a small saucepan, mix together brown sugar, cider vinegar, ketchup, chili sauce, Worcestershire sauce, lemon juice, onion, dry mustard, and 1 clove garlic. Simmer over medium-low heat, uncovered, for 1 hour. Reserve a small amount for basting; the remainder is a dipping sauce.

4. Preheat grill for medium heat.

5. Place ribs on grill. Grill, covered, for about 12 minutes, basting with the reserved sauce, until nicely browned and glazed. Serve with remaining sauce for dipping.

Southern Grilled Barbecued Ribs

Makes: 8 servings

Preparation: 20 minutes

Cooking: 1 hour 30 minutes

Ready In: 1 hour 50 minutes

Submitted by: **Boo**

"These ribs will have the smoky flavor without all the grilling time. It takes just 30 minutes on the grill to give the ribs that smoky flavor Southerners expect. You can use this recipe for spare ribs too, just bake for 15 minutes longer."

INGREDIENTS

4 pounds baby back pork ribs

2/3 cup water

1/3 cup red wine vinegar

1 cup ketchup

1 cup water

1/2 cup cider vinegar

1/3 cup Worcestershire sauce

1/4 cup prepared mustard

4 tablespoons butter

1/2 cup packed brown sugar

1 teaspoon hot pepper sauce

1/8 teaspoon salt

DIRECTIONS

1. Preheat oven to 350°F (175°C). Place ribs in two 10x15 inch roasting pans. Pour water and red wine vinegar into a bowl, and stir. Pour diluted vinegar over ribs and cover with foil. Bake in the preheated oven for 45 minutes. Baste the ribs with their juices halfway through cooking.

2. In a medium saucepan, mix together ketchup, water, vinegar, Worcestershire sauce, mustard, butter, brown sugar, hot pepper sauce, and salt; bring to a boil. Reduce heat to low, cover, and simmer barbeque sauce for 1 hour.

3. Preheat grill for medium heat.

4. Lightly oil preheated grill. Transfer ribs from the oven to the grill, discarding cooking liquid. Grill over medium heat for 15 minutes, turning ribs once. Baste ribs generously with barbeque sauce, and grill 8 minutes. Turn ribs, baste again with barbeque sauce, and grill 8 minutes.

Tangy BBQ Ribs

Submitted by: **Larry Aman**

Makes: 8 servings

Preparation: 10 minutes

Cooking: 2 hours 45 minutes

Ready In: 2 hours 55 minutes

"Country-style bbq pork ribs grilled and then baked in a delicious glaze of molasses, honey, and ketchup."

INGREDIENTS

8 country style pork ribs

1 cup honey

1 cup ketchup

2 tablespoons molasses

1 (18 ounce) bottle barbeque sauce

DIRECTIONS

1. Preheat grill for medium-high heat.

2. Lightly oil grill grate. Grill ribs for 12 minutes, turning once during cooking. Transfer ribs to an 11x16 inch baking dish.

3. Preheat oven to 350°F (175°C). In a large bowl, stir together the honey, ketchup, molasses, and barbecue sauce.

4. Bake ribs, uncovered, for 1 hour. Remove from the oven, and drain fat. Coat ribs with the honey sauce. Continue baking for another 1½ hours, or until ribs are tender.

Garlic Cajun Ribs

Submitted by: **John Samples**

Makes: 8 servings

Preparation: 15 minutes

Cooking: 45 minutes

Ready In: 1 hour 15 minutes

"This is a tasty, treaty baby back ribs recipe, and it's real easy to prepare. Serve the remaining glaze with the ribs."

INGREDIENTS

1½ gallons water

2 tablespoons minced garlic

4 tablespoons Cajun seasoning

4 tablespoons seasoned salt

4 pounds pork baby back ribs

1 (18 ounce) bottle barbeque sauce

2 tablespoons minced garlic

2 tablespoons Cajun seasoning

2 tablespoons seasoned salt

6 tablespoons Worcestershire sauce

DIRECTIONS

1. Preheat grill for medium heat.

2. In a large pot, bring the water to a boil. Season boiling water with 2 tablespoons garlic, 4 tablespoons Cajun-style seasoning, and 4 tablespoons seasoned salt. Boil ribs in seasoned water for 15 to 20 minutes.

3. In a mixing bowl, mix together barbeque sauce, 2 tablespoons garlic, 2 tablespoons Cajun-style seasoning, 2 tablespoons seasoned salt, and Worcestershire sauce.

4. Place ribs in large baking dishes, and apply a generous amount of the barbeque sauce mixture to the ribs. Set aside for 10 to 15 minutes to marinate.

5. Grill the ribs for 7 to 12 minutes per side, until nicely browned.

Indonesian Pork Satay

Submitted by: **Debbie**

Makes: 4 servings

Preparation: 30 minutes

Cooking: 15 minutes

Ready In: 6 hours 45 minutes

"Serve with dipping sauce on the side. Chicken, beef, or lamb can also be used instead of pork."

INGREDIENTS

2 cloves garlic

1/2 cup chopped green onions

1 tablespoon chopped fresh ginger root

1 cup roasted, salted Spanish peanuts

2 tablespoons lemon juice

2 tablespoons honey

1/2 cup soy sauce

2 teaspoons crushed coriander seed

1 teaspoon red pepper flakes

1/2 cup chicken broth

1/2 cup melted butter

11/2 pounds pork tenderloin, cut into 1 inch cubes

skewers

DIRECTIONS

1. In a food processor, process garlic, green onions, ginger, peanuts, lemon juice, honey, soy sauce, coriander, and red pepper flakes. Puree until almost smooth. Pour in broth and butter, and mix again.

2. Place pork cubes in a large resealable plastic bag, and pour mixture over meat. Marinate in the refrigerator for 6 hours, or overnight.

3. Preheat grill for medium heat. Remove pork cubes from bag, and thread onto skewers. In a small saucepan, boil the marinade for 5 minutes. Reserve a small amount of the marinade for basting, and set the remainder aside to serve as a dipping sauce.

4. Lightly oil preheated grill. Grill for 10 to 15 minutes, or until well browned, turning and brushing frequently with cooked marinade. Serve with dipping sauce.

Thai Pork Satay

Submitted by: **Paul**

Makes: 4 servings

Preparation: 45 minutes

Cooking: 10 minutes

Ready In: 55 minutes

"This is a wonderful pork shish kabob with a Thai flavor. I took this on a church campout and it was a huge hit."

INGREDIENTS

1/4 cup crunchy peanut butter

1/4 cup finely chopped green onions

2 tablespoons soy sauce

2 tablespoons lemon juice

1 1/2 tablespoons brown sugar

2 teaspoons minced garlic

1 teaspoon ground coriander

1/8 teaspoon ground cayenne pepper

1 pound pork tenderloin, cubed

1 (8 ounce) can water chestnuts, drained

1 medium green bell pepper, cut into 2 inch pieces

1 medium red bell pepper, cut into 2 inch pieces

1 small sweet onion, quartered

skewers

DIRECTIONS

1. In a medium bowl, mix peanut butter, green onions, soy sauce, lemon juice, brown sugar, garlic, coriander, and cayenne pepper; add pork, and stir to coat. Cover, and marinate in the refrigerator at least 30 minutes.

2. Preheat grill for high heat. Thread marinated pork, water chestnuts, green bell pepper, red bell pepper, and sweet onion alternately onto skewers. Transfer remaining marinade to a small saucepan, bring to a boil, and cook for several minutes.

3. Lightly oil grate. Cook skewers for 10 minutes, or to desired doneness. Turn skewers while grilling to cook evenly, and brush with boiled marinade during last few minutes.

Ham and Pineapple Kabobs

Submitted by: **Lindsay Perejma**

Makes: 4 servings

Preparation: 15 minutes

Cooking: 8 minutes

Ready In: 23 minutes

"Cooked ham and pineapple chunks threaded onto skewers and coated with a zesty, sweet glaze."

INGREDIENTS

3 tablespoons brown sugar

2 tablespoons distilled white vinegar

1 tablespoon vegetable oil

1 teaspoon prepared mustard

3/4 pound cooked ham, cut into 1 inch cubes

1 (15 ounce) can pineapple chunks, drained

skewers

DIRECTIONS

1. Preheat grill for high heat.

2. In a medium bowl, mix together brown sugar, vinegar, vegetable oil, and mustard. Thread ham and pineapple chunks alternately onto skewers.

3. Lightly oil grill grate. Place skewers on the prepared grill, and brush liberally with the brown sugar mixture. Cook for 6 to 8 minutes, turning frequently and basting often. Serve when heated through and richly glazed.

Souvlaki

Submitted by: **Abby Benner**

Makes: 12 servings

Preparation: 30 minutes

Cooking: 15 minutes

Ready In: 2 hours 45 minutes

"Souvlaki is a Greek specialty made with tender cuts of meat. In this pork recipe, the meat is marinated in a lemony olive oil mixture. Serve with rice pilaf and a Greek salad."

INGREDIENTS

1 lemon, juiced

1/4 cup olive oil

1/4 cup soy sauce

1 teaspoon dried oregano

3 cloves garlic, crushed

4 pounds pork tenderloin, cut into 1 inch cubes

2 medium yellow onions, cut into 1 inch pieces

2 green bell peppers, cut into 1 inch pieces

skewers

DIRECTIONS

1. In a large glass bowl, mix together lemon juice, olive oil, soy sauce, oregano, and garlic; add pork, onions, and green peppers, and stir to coat. Cover, and refrigerate for 2 to 3 hours.

2. Preheat grill for medium-high heat. Thread pork, peppers, and onions onto skewers.

3. Lightly oil grate. Cook for 10 to 15 minutes, or to desired doneness, turning skewers frequently for even cooking.

Wisconsin Bratwurst

Submitted by: **Bob Cody**

Makes: 10 servings

Preparation: 10 minutes

Cooking: 35 minutes

Ready In: 45 minutes

"This is the only way to cook bratwurst in Wisconsin. The brats are incredibly tasty! If you can get fresh bratwurst from a sausage shop, do it... it is worth the extra cost. Serve with brown mustard on substantial hoagie rolls, never on hot dog buns. Mustard is important and must always be stone ground. Add warm sauerkraut and ketchup, if you like. Chow down! Think about those Wisconsin summers! Listen to some polka!"

INGREDIENTS

2 pounds fresh bratwurst sausages

2 onions, thinly sliced

1 cup butter

6 (12 fluid ounce) cans or bottles beer

1½ teaspoons ground black pepper

10 hoagie rolls

DIRECTIONS

1. Prick bratwurst with fork to prevent them from exploding as they cook. Place in a large stock pot with the onions, butter, and beer. Place pot over medium heat, and simmer for 15 to 20 minutes.

2. Preheat grill for medium-high heat.

3. Lightly oil grate. Cook bratwurst on preheated grill for 10 to 14 minutes, turning occasionally to brown evenly. Serve hot off the grill with onions on hoagie rolls.

Pork Apple Burgers

Submitted by: **Kevin**

Makes: 8 servings

Preparation: 20 minutes

Cooking: 10 minutes

Ready In: 30 minutes

"A sweet and savory taste treat your family is sure to enjoy. Serve with a slice of pineapple on a toasted bun."

INGREDIENTS

2 pounds ground pork

1 Granny Smith apple - peeled, cored and chopped

1 sweet onion, finely chopped

3 cloves garlic, minced

1/4 cup teriyaki sauce

1 egg

8 hamburger buns

1 (20 ounce) can sliced pineapple, drained

DIRECTIONS

1. Preheat grill for medium-high heat.

2. In a large bowl, mix together ground pork, apple, onion, garlic, teriyaki sauce, and egg. If too dry, add some juice from the can of pineapple slices. Form into eight patties.

3. Lightly oil grill grate. Grill pork burgers for 10 minutes, or until well done. Toast buns on grill. Serve burgers on toasted buns topped with pineapple slices.

poultry

Marinades, spice rubs, and smoke turn a bland breast or a thigh into something worthy of a grand occasion. See the hints at the beginning of this book for grilling with indirect heat, and your bone-in chicken pieces will never again suffer from that common chicken ailment of "burned on the outside, raw on the inside."

Unbelievable Chicken

Submitted by: **Ruthie Crickmer**

Makes: 6 servings

Preparation: 15 minutes

Cooking: 20 minutes

Ready In: 9 hours

"This unusual combination of common ingredients is fabulous! Everyone who tastes it asks me to share the recipe. You will love it and the many compliments you get - I promise!"

INGREDIENTS

1/4 cup cider vinegar

3 tablespoons prepared coarse-ground mustard

3 cloves garlic, peeled and minced

1 lime, juiced

1/2 lemon, juiced

1/2 cup brown sugar

1 1/2 teaspoons salt

ground black pepper to taste

6 tablespoons olive oil

6 skinless, boneless chicken breast halves

DIRECTIONS

1. In a large glass bowl, mix the cider vinegar, mustard, garlic, lime juice, lemon juice, brown sugar, salt, and pepper. Whisk in the olive oil. Place chicken in the mixture. Cover, and marinate 8 hours, or overnight.

2. Preheat an outdoor grill for high heat.

3. Lightly oil the grill grate. Place chicken on the prepared grill, and cook 6 to 8 minutes per side, until juices run clear. Discard marinade.

Honey Mustard Grilled Chicken

Submitted by: **Connie**

Makes: 4 servings

Preparation: 15 minutes

Cooking: 20 minutes

Ready In: 35 minutes

"'If ye have faith as a grain of mustard seed', ye shall make and enjoy this simple, tangy, delicious grilled chicken dish!"

INGREDIENTS

⅓ cup Dijon mustard

¼ cup honey

2 tablespoons mayonnaise

1 teaspoon steak sauce

4 skinless, boneless chicken breast halves

DIRECTIONS

1. Preheat the grill for medium heat.

2. In a shallow bowl, mix the mustard, honey, mayonnaise, and steak sauce. Set aside a small amount of the honey mustard sauce for basting, and dip the chicken into the remaining sauce to coat.

3. Lightly oil the grill grate. Grill chicken over indirect heat for 18 to 20 minutes, turning occasionally, or until juices run clear. Baste occasionally with the reserved sauce during the last 10 minutes. Watch carefully to prevent burning!

Marinated Rosemary Lemon Chicken

Makes: 4 servings

Preparation: 15 minutes

Cooking: 15 minutes

Ready In: 8 hours 30 minutes

Submitted by: **Barbara Edwards**

"Perfect for the summer barbecue! Serve with rice, a light pasta salad, or grilled corn. Great summer eating!"

INGREDIENTS

1/2 cup lemon juice

1/8 cup olive oil

2 tablespoons dried rosemary

4 skinless, boneless chicken breast halves

1 lemon, sliced

DIRECTIONS

1. In a large resealable plastic bag, mix the lemon juice, olive oil, and rosemary. Place the chicken and lemon slices in the bag. Seal, and shake to coat. Marinate in the refrigerator 8 hours or overnight.

2. Preheat the grill for high heat.

3. Lightly oil the grill grate. Discard marinade, and grill chicken 8 minutes per side, or until juices run clear. Don't worry about the rosemary sticking to the chicken, it tastes great when it's grilled. If you use fresh rosemary sprigs, throw the stems onto the coals - they give the chicken even more of a smoky rosemary flavor!

Bessy's Zesty Grilled Garlic-Herb Chicken

Submitted by: **Bessy Thompson**

Makes: 4 servings

Preparation: 15 minutes

Cooking: 40 minutes

Ready In: 1 hour 15 minutes

"Though seemingly unconventional, this recipe will surely please anyone. The combination of exotic ingredients comes together perfectly to form an altogether delicious grilled chicken."

INGREDIENTS

4 skinless, boneless chicken breast halves

1 cup extra virgin olive oil

1/2 cup white sugar

1/2 tablespoon honey

1/2 teaspoon saffron

4 cloves garlic, minced

1 teaspoon dried basil

1 teaspoon dried thyme

1 teaspoon cayenne pepper

1 teaspoon salt

1/2 teaspoon dried oregano

1/4 teaspoon dried parsley

1 pinch dried sage

DIRECTIONS

1. Place chicken in a shallow dish. In a medium bowl, mix together the olive oil, sugar, honey, saffron, garlic, basil, thyme, cayenne pepper, salt, oregano, parsley, and sage. Pour the mixture over the chicken. Cover, and marinate 20 to 25 minutes in the refrigerator.

2. Preheat the grill for medium heat.

3. Lightly oil the grill grate. Discard marinade, and place chicken on the grill. Cook for 10 minutes on each side, or until juices run clear.

Favorite Barbecue Chicken

Submitted by: **Amanda Anne**

Makes: 2 servings

Preparation: 5 minutes

Cooking: 35 minutes

Ready In: 40 minutes

"A not-too-sweet, not-too-tangy barbecue sauce that everyone loves. Finishes in almost a glaze and would also be great on pork chops or ribs."

INGREDIENTS

1½ tablespoons olive oil

¼ cup diced onion

2 cloves garlic, minced

5 tablespoons ketchup

3 tablespoons honey

3 tablespoons brown sugar

2 tablespoons apple cider vinegar

1 tablespoon Worcestershire sauce

salt and pepper to taste

2 skinless, boneless chicken breast halves

DIRECTIONS

1. Preheat grill for medium-high heat.

2. Heat olive oil in a skillet over medium heat. Saute onion and garlic until tender. Stir in ketchup, honey, brown sugar, apple cider vinegar, Worcestershire sauce, salt, and pepper. Cook for a few minutes to thicken sauce. Remove from heat, and allow to cool.

3. Lightly oil the grill grate. Dip chicken in sauce, and turn to coat. Cook on grill for 10 to 15 minutes, turning once. Move chicken to the skillet with sauce. Simmer over medium heat for about 5 minutes on each side.

Grilled Chicken Breast with Cucumber and Pepper Relish

Submitted by: **Fiona Karoly**

Makes: 4 servings

Preparation: 15 minutes

Cooking: 15 minutes

Ready In: 1 hour 30 minutes

"A great dish for entertaining outdoors."

INGREDIENTS

1 cucumber - peeled, seeded and chopped

1 tablespoon chopped fresh parsley

1/8 cup chopped red onion

1/2 cup chopped yellow bell pepper

1/4 teaspoon crushed red pepper flakes

1/2 teaspoon ground cumin

1/8 teaspoon chili powder

2 tablespoons olive oil

4 skinless, boneless chicken breasts

DIRECTIONS

1. In a medium bowl, prepare the relish by mixing together the cucumber, parsley, chopped onion, bell pepper, and red pepper flakes. Set aside.

2. In a small bowl, mix the cumin and chili powder with the olive oil. Rub the mixture onto the chicken, and place in a shallow dish. Marinate in the refrigerator at least 1 hour.

3. Prepare the grill for medium heat.

4. Lightly oil the grill grate. Grill chicken 8 minutes per side, or until juices run clear. Serve with cucumber relish.

Cajun Chicken

Submitted by: **Wood Halsey**

Makes: 10 servings

Preparation: 15 minutes

Cooking: 15 minutes

Ready In: 1 hour

"Cajun style grilled chicken breasts for varied meals such as Caesar salad, sandwiches, and a dinner entree! Cajun Chicken can be served hot or cold."

INGREDIENTS

2 cups vegetable oil

2 tablespoons Cajun seasoning

2 tablespoons dried Italian-style seasoning

garlic powder to taste

2 tablespoons lemon pepper

10 skinless, boneless chicken breast halves - pounded to 1/2 inch thickness

DIRECTIONS

1. In a large shallow dish, mix the oil, Cajun seasoning, Italian seasoning, garlic powder, and lemon pepper. Place the chicken in the dish, and turn to coat with the mixture. Cover, and refrigerate for 1/2 hour.

2. Preheat the grill for high heat.

3. Lightly oil the grill grate. Drain chicken, and discard marinade. Place chicken on hot grill and cook for 6 to 8 minutes on each side, or until juices run clear.

Jay's Jerk Chicken

Submitted by: **R.H. Solomon**

Makes: 4 servings

Preparation: 15 minutes

Cooking: 30 minutes

Ready In: 4 hours 45 minutes

"This is one of my nephew's favorite grilled recipes. Jerk means Jamaican barbecue. This well rounded flavor of sweet, hot, herbal and spicy chicken can be served with rice, beans or pasta. Or just make a chicken sandwich out of it! I also add garlic and a kiwi to the marinade."

INGREDIENTS

6 green onions, chopped

1 onion, chopped

1 jalapeno pepper, seeded and minced

3/4 cup soy sauce

1/2 cup distilled white vinegar

1/4 cup vegetable oil

2 tablespoons brown sugar

1 tablespoon chopped fresh thyme

1/2 teaspoon ground cloves

1/2 teaspoon ground nutmeg

1/2 teaspoon ground allspice

11/2 pounds skinless, boneless chicken breast halves

DIRECTIONS

1. In a food processor or blender, combine the green onions, onion, jalapeno pepper, soy sauce, vinegar, vegetable oil, brown sugar, thyme, cloves, nutmeg and allspice. Mix for about 15 seconds.

2. Place the chicken in a medium bowl, and coat with the marinade. Refrigerate for 4 to 6 hours, or overnight.

3. Preheat grill for high heat.

4. Lightly oil grill grate. Cook chicken on the prepared grill 6 to 8 minutes, or until juices run clear.

Jalapeno Chicken II

Submitted by: **Cristi Rhymes**

Makes: 6 servings

Preparation: 25 minutes

Cooking: 20 minutes

Ready In: 2 hours 45 minutes

"Stuffed jalapeno peppers are wrapped in marinated chicken breasts. Tasty bacon seals the deal!"

INGREDIENTS

6 skinless, boneless chicken breast halves - pounded to 1/4 inch thickness

1 (16 ounce) bottle Italian dressing

3 fresh jalapeno peppers, halved lengthwise and seeded

1 (3 ounce) package cream cheese, softened

6 slices bacon

toothpicks

DIRECTIONS

1. Place chicken breasts in a dish with the Italian dressing. Cover, and marinate in the refrigerator at least 2 hours.

2. Preheat the grill for high heat.

3. Stuff each jalapeno half with cream cheese. Roll chicken breasts around jalapeno peppers. Wrap each chicken breast with a slice of bacon. Secure with toothpicks.

4. Lightly oil the grill grate. Arrange wrapped chicken breasts on the prepared grill. Cook for 20 minutes, turning frequently, or until bacon is browned and the chicken juices run clear.

Spicy Grilled Chicken

Submitted by: **Jenn H.**

Makes: 6 servings

Preparation: 15 minutes

Cooking: 15 minutes

Ready In: 1 hour 30 minutes

"This recipe is very easy to make! Perfect for summer barbeques, but it can be broiled indoors anytime. Always a favorite!"

INGREDIENTS

1/3 cup vegetable oil

2 tablespoons lime juice

1/2 teaspoon grated lime zest

2 cloves crushed garlic

1 1/2 teaspoons fresh oregano

1/4 teaspoon red pepper flakes

1 teaspoon salt

1/4 teaspoon ground black pepper

6 skinless, boneless chicken breast halves

DIRECTIONS

1. In a shallow glass dish, mix the oil, lime juice, lime zest, garlic, oregano, red pepper flakes, salt, and black pepper. Add chicken, and turn to coat. Cover, and marinate in the refrigerator for 1 hour, turning occasionally.

2. Preheat grill for medium-high heat.

3. Lightly oil the grill grate. Drain and discard marinade. Grill chicken for 6 to 8 minutes each side, or until juices run clear.

Hawaiian Chicken I

Submitted by: **Barbara Childers**

Makes: 6 servings

Preparation: 5 minutes

Cooking: 25 minutes

Ready In: 8 hours 30 minutes

"This was given to me by my best friend years ago and is a favorite of our family!"

INGREDIENTS

6 skinless, boneless chicken breast halves

2 cups teriyaki sauce, divided

6 pineapple rings

1/2 cup butter, melted

3/4 cup packed brown sugar

3/4 cup soy sauce

3/4 cup unsweetened pineapple juice

6 tablespoons Worcestershire sauce

DIRECTIONS

1. Place the chicken breast halves in a dish with the 1½ cups of teriyaki sauce. Cover and refrigerate 8 hours or overnight.

2. Preheat a grill for high heat.

3. Lightly oil the grill grate. Place chicken breasts on grill, and discard marinade. Cook for 8 minutes per side, or until juices run clear. Brush with the remaining teriyaki sauce during the last 5 minutes. When almost done, place one pineapple ring on top of each breast, and brush with melted butter.

4. In a small saucepan over medium heat, mix the brown sugar, soy sauce, pineapple juice, and Worcestershire sauce. Cook, stirring occasionally, until sugar is dissolved. Serve with chicken for dipping!

Grilled Asian Chicken

Submitted by: **Janet M.**

Makes: 4 servings

Preparation: 15 minutes

Cooking: 15 minutes

Ready In: 50 minutes

"Great for last minute company or a quick dinner by rounding it out with a baked potato and tossed salad."

INGREDIENTS

1/4 cup soy sauce

4 teaspoons sesame oil

2 tablespoons honey

3 slices fresh ginger root

2 cloves garlic, crushed

4 skinless, boneless chicken breast halves

DIRECTIONS

1. In a small microwave-safe bowl, combine the soy sauce, oil, honey, ginger root, and garlic. Heat in microwave on medium for 1 minute, then stir. Heat again for 30 seconds, watching closely to prevent boiling.

2. Place chicken breasts in a shallow dish. Pour soy sauce mixture over, and set aside to marinate for 15 minutes.

3. Preheat a grill for medium-high heat. Drain marinade from chicken into a small saucepan. Bring to a boil, and simmer over medium heat for 5 minutes. Set aside for basting.

4. Lightly oil the grill grate. Cook chicken on the prepared grill 6 to 8 minutes per side, or until juices run clear. Baste frequently with remaining marinade. Chicken will turn a beautiful golden brown.

Easy Grilled Chicken Teriyaki

Submitted by: **T's Mom**

Makes: 4 servings

Preparation: 15 minutes

Cooking: 15 minutes

Ready In: 24 hours 30 minutes

"Chicken breasts marinated in teriyaki sauce, lemon, garlic, and sesame oil, then grilled to a tasty finish. Very easy and great for a hot summer's evening. Leftovers are great on a green salad or sandwich. Be sure to grill very hot and very fast!!"

INGREDIENTS

4 skinless, boneless chicken breast halves

1 cup teriyaki sauce

1/4 cup lemon juice

2 teaspoons minced fresh garlic

2 teaspoons sesame oil

DIRECTIONS

1. Place chicken, teriyaki sauce, lemon juice, garlic, and sesame oil in a large resealable plastic bag. Seal bag, and shake to coat. Place in refrigerator for 24 hours, turning every so often.

2. Preheat grill for high heat.

3. Lightly oil the grill grate. Remove chicken from bag, discarding any remaining marinade. Grill for 6 to 8 minutes each side, or until juices run clear when chicken is pierced with a fork.

BBQ Miso Chicken

Submitted by: **Eric**

Makes: 6 servings

Preparation: 15 minutes

Cooking: 25 minutes

Ready In: 2 hours 40 minutes

"Boneless chicken marinated in a miso (soy bean paste) sauce and grilled over an open fire. The miso is also mixed with beer, soy sauce, sugar, and sesame oil to give it a complex flavor."

INGREDIENTS

1 cup miso paste

1 cup beer

1 cup low sodium soy sauce

1 cup white sugar

2 teaspoons sesame oil

$1/8$ teaspoon cayenne pepper

$2 1/2$ pounds skinless, boneless chicken breast halves

DIRECTIONS

1. In a large bowl, combine the miso paste, beer, soy sauce, sugar, sesame oil, and cayenne pepper. Stir until the miso and sugar are completely dissolved. Set aside ½ cup of the sauce for basting during grilling. Submerge the chicken in the remaining marinade, cover bowl, and refrigerate for at least 2 hours.

2. Preheat grill for medium-high heat.

3. Lightly oil the grill grate. Remove the chicken from the marinade, and discard marinade. Grill chicken for 6 to 8 minutes per side, basting during the last few minutes with the reserved sauce. The chicken is done when the juices run clear.

Tandoori Chicken II

Submitted by: **Bonnie**

Makes: 4 servings

Preparation: 15 minutes

Cooking: 15 minutes

Ready In: 50 minutes

"A paste made from a combination of spices and dried peppers is the secret to this spicy grilled chicken recipe. No long marinating time is required; the chicken can be prepared in the time it takes to get the coals hot."

INGREDIENTS

1/2 teaspoon curry powder

1/2 teaspoon red pepper flakes

1/2 teaspoon kosher salt

1/4 teaspoon ground ginger

1/4 teaspoon paprika

1/4 teaspoon ground cinnamon

1/4 teaspoon ground turmeric

2 tablespoons water

4 skinless, boneless chicken breast halves

DIRECTIONS

1. Preheat grill for high heat.

2. In a medium bowl, mix curry powder, red pepper flakes, salt, ginger, paprika, cinnamon, and turmeric with water to form a smooth paste. Rub paste into chicken breasts, and place them on a plate. Cover, and allow to marinate for 20 minutes.

3. Brush grate with oil. Place chicken on the grill, and cook 6 to 8 minutes on each side, until juices run clear when pierced with a fork.

Marinated Turkey Breast

Submitted by: **Danielle**

Makes: 12 servings

Preparation: 20 minutes

Cooking: 30 minutes

Ready In: 5 hours

"This recipe came from my mother. These always turn out juicy and tender no matter how long my husband leaves them on the grill! Easy to prepare, but it's always best when marinated for at least 4 hours."

INGREDIENTS

2 cloves garlic, peeled and minced

1 tablespoon finely chopped fresh basil

1/2 teaspoon ground black pepper

2 (3 pound) boneless turkey breast halves

6 whole cloves

1/4 cup vegetable oil

1/4 cup soy sauce

2 tablespoons lemon juice

1 tablespoon brown sugar

DIRECTIONS

1. In a small bowl, mix together the garlic, basil, and pepper. Rub over the turkey breasts. Insert one clove into each end of the turkey breasts, and one in the center.

2. In a large shallow dish, blend vegetable oil, soy sauce, lemon juice, and brown sugar. Place the breasts in the dish, and turn to coat. Cover, and marinate in the refrigerator at least 4 hours.

3. Preheat grill for high heat.

4. Lightly oil the grill grate. Discard marinade, place turkey breasts on the grill. Close the lid, and grill turkey breasts about 15 minutes on each side, or to an internal temperature of 170°F (68°C).

Honey Smoked Turkey

Submitted by: **Tammie**

Makes: 1 (12 pound) turkey

Preparation: 30 minutes

Cooking: 3 hours 15 minutes

Ready In: 3 hours 45 minutes

"Sweet and light, this is the easiest way to cook a big bird! It will be the best turkey you have ever had. The breast is moist and juicy, and the honey makes a great thin sauce. I hope you enjoy it as much as my friends and family do when I make it. I never have any leftovers! Enjoy!"

INGREDIENTS

1 (12 pound) whole turkey

2 tablespoons chopped fresh sage

2 tablespoons ground black pepper

2 tablespoons celery salt

2 tablespoons chopped fresh basil

2 tablespoons vegetable oil

1 (12 ounce) jar honey

1/2 pound mesquite wood chips

DIRECTIONS

1. Preheat grill for high heat. If you are using a charcoal grill, use about twice the normal amount of charcoal. Soak wood chips in a pan of water, and set next to the grill.

2. Remove neck and giblets from turkey. Rinse the bird and pat dry. Place in a large disposable roasting pan.

3. In a medium bowl, mix together sage, ground black pepper, celery salt, basil, and vegetable oil. Pour mixture evenly over the turkey. Turn the turkey breast side down in the pan, and tent loosely with aluminum foil.

4. Place the roasting pan on the preheated grill. Throw a handful of the wood chips onto the coals. Close the lid, and cook for 1 hour.

5. Throw about 2 more handfuls of soaked wood chips on the fire. Drizzle 1/2 the honey over the bird, and replace the foil. Close the lid of the grill, and continue cooking 1 1/2 to 2 hours, or until internal temperature reaches 180°F (80°C) in the thickest part of the thigh.

6. Uncover turkey, and carefully turn it breast side up in the roasting pan. Baste with remaining honey. Leave the turkey uncovered, and cook 15 minutes. The cooked honey will be very dark.

Turkey in a Smoker

Submitted by: **Doug Kacsir**

Makes: 1 (10 pound) turkey

Preparation: 20 minutes

Cooking: 10 hours

Ready In: 10 hours 20 minutes

"This is a great recipe for smoked turkey. A barbecue grill is nearly impossible to cook a large bird. A smoker is best for this. I prefer hickory chips or hickory wood. Hickory generates a more even smokiness than other woods, and it does not matter whether the wood is green or seasoned. Mesquite, if not well seasoned, will generate a creosote type coating because of the sap that oozes out of the wood while cooking."

INGREDIENTS

1 (10 pound) whole turkey, neck and giblets removed

4 cloves garlic, crushed

2 tablespoons seasoned salt

1/2 cup butter

2 (12 fluid ounce) cans cola-flavored carbonated beverage

1 apple, quartered

1 onion, quartered

1 tablespoon garlic powder

1 tablespoon salt

1 tablespoon ground black pepper

DIRECTIONS

1. Preheat smoker to 225 to 250°F (110 to 120°C).

2. Rinse turkey under cold water, and pat dry. Rub the crushed garlic over the outside of the bird, and sprinkle with seasoned salt. Place in a disposable roasting pan. Fill turkey cavity with butter, cola, apple, onion, garlic powder, salt, and ground black pepper. Cover loosely with foil.

3. Smoke at 225 to 250°F (110 to 120°C) for 10 hours, or until internal temperature reaches 180°F (80°C) when measured in the thickest part of the thigh. Baste the bird every 1 to 2 hours with the juices from the bottom of the roasting pan.

Beer Butt Chicken

Submitted by: **Barrie Tapp**

Makes: 8 servings

Preparation: 30 minutes

Cooking: 3 hours

Ready In: 4 hours

"A whole chicken is seasoned and slowly cooked on the grill. This is a bit unorthodox, but the end result is moist, flavorful, and amazing. All you'll need is some chicken, butter, beer, and seasonings."

INGREDIENTS

1 cup butter

2 tablespoons garlic salt

2 tablespoons paprika

salt and pepper to taste

1 (12 fluid ounce) can beer

1 (4 pound) whole chicken

DIRECTIONS

1. Preheat an outdoor grill for low heat.

2. In a small skillet, melt ½ cup butter. Mix in 1 tablespoon garlic salt, 1 tablespoon paprika, salt, and pepper.

3. Discard ½ the beer, leaving the remainder in the can. Add remaining butter, garlic salt, paprika, and desired amount of salt and pepper to beer can. Place can on a disposable baking sheet. Set chicken on can, inserting can into the cavity of the chicken. Baste chicken with the melted, seasoned butter.

4. Place baking sheet with beer and chicken on the prepared grill. Cook over low heat for about 3 hours, or until internal temperature of chicken reaches 180°F (80°C).

Beer Chicken

Submitted by: **Tom Bartlett**

Makes: 4 servings

Preparation: 15 minutes

Cooking: 1 hour

Ready In: 1 hour 15 minutes

"This is a chicken recipe from ranch hand trail cooks. The garlic on the coals trick will probably bring your neighbors over. So, beware, and cook plenty!!"

INGREDIENTS

1 (12 fluid ounce) can or bottle beer

1/2 cup butter

2 tablespoons garlic powder

1 tablespoon seasoned pepper

1 (3 pound) chicken, split in half lengthwise

garlic powder to taste

ground black pepper to taste

1 pinch seasoned salt

DIRECTIONS

1. Preheat grill for high heat.

2. In a microwave-safe bowl, combine the beer, butter, 1 tablespoon garlic powder and seasoned pepper. Heat in the microwave for 2 minutes, or until butter is melted and mixture is hot. Set aside.

3. Season chicken generously with the garlic powder, ground black pepper and seasoned salt to taste.

4. Brush the grilling surface with oil. Place chicken onto the grill bone side down. Close the lid, and cook for about 45 minutes, or until the chicken skin is starting to blister.

5. Turn the chicken over, so it is bone side up. They will be black and charred, but the chicken meat will be fine. Pierce the membrane of the bone with a fork, and ladle some of the beer mixture into the 'cup' formed by the bones. Throw a teaspoon or so of garlic powder on the coals, close the lid, and seal the vents.

6. Repeat ladling the beer mixture into the chicken, and throwing garlic powder onto the coals every 5 minutes, until the mixture is gone. The chicken should be tender and the juices should run clear.

Greek Chicken

Submitted by: **Karen**

Makes: 8 servings

Preparation: 15 minutes

Cooking: 30 minutes

Ready In: 8 hours 45 minutes

"A very good light summer dish. I serve it with sliced tomatoes, feta cheese, and garlic bread."

INGREDIENTS

1/2 cup olive oil

3 cloves garlic, chopped

1 tablespoon chopped fresh rosemary

1 tablespoon chopped fresh thyme

1 tablespoon chopped fresh oregano

2 lemons, juiced

1 (4 pound) chicken, cut into pieces

DIRECTIONS

1. In a glass dish, mix the olive oil, garlic, rosemary, thyme, oregano, and lemon juice. Place the chicken pieces in the mixture, cover, and marinate in the refrigerator 8 hours or overnight.

2. Preheat grill for high heat.

3. Lightly oil the grill grate. Place chicken on the grill, and discard the marinade. Cook chicken pieces up to 15 minutes per side, until juices run clear. Smaller pieces will not take as long.

Barbequed Thai Style Chicken

Submitted by: **Skye**

Makes: 6 servings

Preparation: 15 minutes

Cooking: 30 minutes

Ready In: 3 hours 45 minutes

"Rich, exciting flavors make this grilled chicken an exotic favorite. Arrange cooked chicken pieces on a serving platter lined with salad greens or a banana leaf. Garnish with cilantro (coriander) sprigs and serve with salad or steamed rice."

INGREDIENTS

1 bunch fresh cilantro with roots

3 cloves garlic, peeled

3 small red hot chile peppers, seeded and chopped

1 teaspoon ground turmeric

1 teaspoon curry powder

1 tablespoon white sugar

1 pinch salt

3 tablespoons fish sauce

1 (3 pound) chicken, cut into pieces

1/4 cup coconut milk

DIRECTIONS

1. Cut cilantro roots off at the stem, and mince thoroughly. Set aside a few leaves for garnish. In a blender or food processor, combine cilantro roots and leaves, garlic, chile peppers, turmeric, curry powder, sugar, and salt. Process to a coarse paste. Pour in fish sauce, and blend until smooth.

2. Place chicken in a large shallow dish. Rub with the cilantro paste. Cover, and marinate in the refrigerator at least 3 hours, or overnight.

3. Preheat grill for high heat.

4. Lightly oil the grill grate. Place chicken on the prepared grill, and brush liberally with coconut milk. Grill chicken 8 to 15 minutes on each side, depending on the size of the pieces. Turn only once, and baste occasionally with coconut milk. Cook until browned and tender, and juices run clear.

Indian Barbeque Chicken

Submitted by: **Karen**

Makes: 6 servings

Preparation: 15 minutes

Cooking: 45 minutes

Ready In: 9 hours

"Marinate the chicken overnight for a deliciously flavorful and tender chicken dish. This is an adaptation of Tandoori style chicken, minus the red coloring."

INGREDIENTS

3 pounds bone-in chicken pieces

3 tablespoons fresh lemon juice

1 tablespoon meat tenderizer

2 cups plain yogurt, divided

3 tablespoons ground cumin

2 tablespoons ground coriander

1/3 cup chopped fresh cilantro

2 teaspoons paprika

1/2 teaspoon ground turmeric

2 teaspoons salt

1 teaspoon ground black pepper

6 cloves garlic, minced

DIRECTIONS

1. Make shallow crosswise slits in the meat of the chicken parts to help absorb more flavor. Mix together the lemon juice and meat tenderizer; rub into the chicken meat. Place chicken into a shallow dish.

2. Place ½ cup yogurt, cumin, coriander, cilantro, paprika, turmeric, salt, pepper, and garlic into a blender or food processor, and blend until smooth. Transfer to a bowl, and stir in remaining 1 ½ cups of yogurt. Pour over the chicken parts, cover, and marinate in the refrigerator for at least 8 hours, or overnight.

3. Preheat grill for medium heat.

4. Lightly oil the grill grate. Remove chicken from the marinade, and discard any remaining marinade. Grill chicken 30 to 45 minutes, turning frequently to prevent burning, until juices run clear. Smaller pieces will finish cooking first.

Thai Grilled Chicken with Sweet Chile Dipping Sauce

Submitted by: **Michelle Chen**

Makes: 4 servings

Preparation: 15 minutes

Cooking: 30 minutes

Ready In: 4 hours 45 minutes

"There are so many versions of this street food found in Thailand. Mine has been in our family for years, and we serve it with a tangy sweet chili sauce that really goes well with this easy dish. We often make a large quantity for parties as all our friends request this."

INGREDIENTS

1/2 cup coconut milk

2 tablespoons fish sauce

2 tablespoons minced garlic

2 tablespoons chopped cilantro

1 teaspoon ground turmeric

1 teaspoon curry powder

1/2 teaspoon white pepper

1/2 (3 pound) chicken, cut into pieces

6 tablespoons rice vinegar

4 tablespoons water

4 tablespoons white sugar

1 teaspoon minced garlic

1/2 teaspoon minced bird's eye chile

1/4 teaspoon salt

DIRECTIONS

1. In a shallow dish, mix together the coconut milk, fish sauce, 2 tablespoons minced garlic, cilantro, turmeric, curry powder, and white pepper. Add chicken, and turn to coat. Cover, and refrigerate for 4 hours or overnight.

2. Preheat grill for high heat.

3. In a saucepan, combine vinegar, water, sugar, 1 teaspoon minced garlic, bird's eye chile, and salt; bring to a boil. Reduce heat to low, and simmer until liquid is reduced, about 5 minutes. Stir sauce from time to time. Remove from heat and allow to cool before use.

4. Lightly oil grill grate. Discard marinade, and place chicken on the grill. Cook for 10 minutes per side, or until slightly charred and juices run clear. Brush with sauce before serving. Serve remaining sauce on the side for dipping.

Chili Chicken

Submitted by: **Margot McKinney**

Makes: 12 servings
Preparation: 10 minutes
Cooking: 20 minutes
Ready In: 1 hour 30 minutes

"A tasty version of drumsticks with a bit of sweetness and spiciness. Thai sweet chili sauce adds an Asian flair."

INGREDIENTS

2 tablespoons honey

5 tablespoons sweet chili sauce

3 tablespoons soy sauce

12 chicken drumsticks, skin removed

DIRECTIONS

1. In a large bowl, mix together the honey, sweet chili sauce, and soy sauce. Set aside a small dish of the marinade for basting. Place chicken drumsticks into the bowl. Cover and refrigerate at least 1 hour.

2. Preheat an outdoor grill for medium-high heat.

3. Lightly oil the grill grate. Arrange drumsticks on the grill. Cook for 10 minutes per side, or until juices run clear. Baste frequently with the reserved sauce during the last 5 minutes.

Big Al's Chicken

Submitted by: **Al Cook**

Makes: 10 servings

Preparation: 15 minutes

Cooking: 20 minutes

Ready In: 8 hours 35 minutes

"An excellent marinade and basting sauce that will amaze you."

INGREDIENTS

1 cup vegetable oil

1/2 cup apple cider vinegar

1/4 cup egg substitute

1 teaspoon garlic powder

1 teaspoon ground paprika

1 teaspoon poultry seasoning

1 tablespoon salt

1 teaspoon black pepper

10 skinless chicken thighs

DIRECTIONS

1. In a jar with a lid, combine the vegetable oil, apple cider vinegar, egg substitute, garlic powder, paprika, poultry seasoning, salt, and pepper. Close the lid, and shake to blend. Place chicken in a shallow glass baking dish. Pour about ¾ of the marinade over it, and reserve the rest for basting. Cover chicken, and refrigerate 8 hours, or overnight.

2. Preheat grill for high heat.

3. Lightly oil the grill grate. Place chicken on the grill, and discard marinade from the dish. Cook the chicken for 10 minutes on each side, or until juices run clear. Brush reserved sauce onto chicken just before serving.

Basic Easy Chicken Wings

Submitted by: **Beth**

Makes: 6 servings

Preparation: 15 minutes

Cooking: 30 minutes

Ready In: 45 minutes

"These are super easy wings that your crowd will love. This recipe will make a dinner for two or hors d'oeuvres for ten. Try your own variations with other sauces, spices, or peppers. Serve with celery sticks and bleu cheese dressing."

INGREDIENTS

3 pounds chicken wings, separated at joints, tips discarded

1/2 cup butter

1 cup hot sauce

1/2 teaspoon cayenne pepper

1/4 teaspoon freshly ground black pepper

DIRECTIONS

1. Preheat grill for high heat.

2. Lightly oil the grill grate. Cook the wings 8 to 12 minutes on each side, until juices run clear. The larger pieces will take slightly longer to cook.

3. Melt the butter in a saucepan, and mix in the hot sauce, cayenne pepper, and black pepper.

4. Place wings in a large container with a secure lid. Pour sauce over the wings, and seal. Shake wings with the sauce until thoroughly coated.

Sweet Spicy Wings

Submitted by: **Lisa I.**

Makes: 12 servings

Preparation: 15 minutes

Cooking: 30 minutes

Ready In: 45 minutes

"Sweet and spicy wings! You can make two batches of the sauce, use one as a marinade before grilling the chicken, and pour the second batch over the chicken after it is grilled. It is not mandatory to do it this way, just better!"

INGREDIENTS

6 pounds chicken wings, separated at joints, tips discarded

1½ cups Louisiana-style hot sauce

¾ cup butter

1 cup honey

1 pinch garlic salt

1 pinch ground black pepper

1 teaspoon cayenne pepper, or to taste

DIRECTIONS

1. Preheat an outdoor grill for high heat.

2. Lightly oil the grill grate. Grill the chicken 8 to 12 minutes on each side, or until juices run clear. (You can deep fry or bake the chicken instead if you want to, but it is best when grilled.) Place chicken in a large roasting pan.

3. In a saucepan over medium heat, mix the hot sauce, butter, honey, garlic salt, black pepper, and cayenne pepper. Simmer about 10 minutes, until blended and heated through. Pour the sauce over the grilled chicken wings and stir to coat.

BBQ Chicken Wings

Submitted by: **Patrick**

Makes: 4 servings

Preparation: 15 minutes

Cooking: 45 minutes

Ready In: 9 hours

"This yummy honey barbeque sauce is great on chicken wings, pork, or short ribs. The soy sauce and oyster sauce hint at an Asian inspiration, while the gin gives it an undeterminable edge."

INGREDIENTS

1/2 cup teriyaki sauce

1 cup oyster sauce

1/4 cup soy sauce

1/4 cup ketchup

2 tablespoons garlic powder

1/4 cup gin

2 dashes liquid smoke flavoring

1/2 cup white sugar

1 1/2 pounds chicken wings, separated at joints, tips discarded

1/4 cup honey

DIRECTIONS

1. In a large bowl, mix the teriyaki sauce, oyster sauce, soy sauce, ketchup, garlic powder, gin, liquid smoke, and sugar. Place the chicken wings in the bowl, cover, and marinate in the refrigerator 8 hours or overnight.

2. Preheat the grill for low heat.

3. Lightly oil the grill grate. Arrange chicken on the grill, and discard the marinade. Grill the chicken wings on one side for 20 minutes, then turn and brush with honey. Continue grilling 25 minutes, or until juices run clear.

Craig's Mystic Wings

Submitted by: **Craig Floyd**

Makes: 6 servings

Preparation: 30 minutes

Cooking: 2 hours

Ready In: 8 hours 30 minutes

"Made with EIGHT habanero chile peppers, these wings are very, very HOT. Wear gloves to chop the peppers. Be warned, and be careful! Serve with ice cold beer and antacid!"

INGREDIENTS

1 (18 ounce) bottle honey teriyaki barbeque sauce

1/2 cup Worcestershire sauce

1/4 cup honey

3 dashes liquid smoke flavoring

1 1/2 tablespoons grated fresh ginger

6 cloves crushed garlic

8 habanero peppers, seeded and minced

4 green chile peppers, chopped

3 tablespoons finely grated raw horseradish

18 chicken wings, separated at joints, tips discarded

DIRECTIONS

1. In a medium saucepan mix together barbeque sauce, Worcestershire sauce, honey, liquid smoke, ginger, garlic, habanero peppers, green chile peppers, and horseradish. Simmer 1 hour over low heat, stirring occasionally.

2. Place chicken wings in a large bowl, and coat with ¾ of the sauce. Cover, and refrigerate for at least 6 hours.

3. Preheat grill for low heat.

4. Lightly oil grate. Discard marinade, and place chicken on the grill. Cook over low heat for 45 minutes to 1 hour, turning occasionally, until juices run clear. Transfer chicken to a slow cooker for serving, and stir in the remaining sauce. Set to the Low setting to keep chicken warm while serving.

Lemon Dijon Wings

Submitted by: **David Sabourin**

Makes: 4 servings

Preparation: 15 minutes

Cooking: 20 minutes

Ready In: 2 hours 35 minutes

"Delicious BBQ wings that are easy to make!"

INGREDIENTS

¼ cup olive oil

1 tablespoon fresh lemon juice

2 tablespoons coarse-grained Dijon mustard

6 cloves garlic, chopped

2 teaspoons salt

1 tablespoon freshly ground black pepper

2 pounds chicken wings, separated at joints, tips discarded

DIRECTIONS

1. In a large bowl, stir together the olive oil, lemon juice, mustard, garlic, salt, and pepper. Add chicken wings, cover, and marinate in the refrigerator for at least 2 hours, stirring occasionally.

2. Preheat grill for high heat. Drain marinade from chicken into a small saucepan. Bring to a boil, and simmer for 5 minutes. Set aside for basting.

3. Lightly oil the grill grate. Grill wings for 10 to 15 minutes, or until juices run clear. Turn frequently and baste with the marinade during the last 5 minutes.

Chicken Kabobs

Submitted by: **Sarah**

Makes: 4 servings

Preparation: 15 minutes

Cooking: 15 minutes

Ready In: 30 minutes

"Here's a colorful, quick, and easy way to do your veggies and chicken on the grill - with no marinating!"

INGREDIENTS

4 skinless, boneless chicken breast halves - cubed

1 large green bell pepper, cut into 2 inch pieces

1 onion, cut into wedges

1 large red bell pepper, cut into 2 inch pieces

1 cup barbeque sauce

skewers

DIRECTIONS

1. Preheat grill for high heat.

2. Thread the chicken, green bell pepper, onion, and red bell pepper pieces onto skewers alternately.

3. Lightly oil the grill grate. Place kabobs on the prepared grill, and brush with barbeque sauce. Cook, turning and brushing with barbeque sauce frequently, for 15 minutes, or until chicken juices run clear.

RamJam Chicken

Submitted by: **Laura Ramanjooloo**

Makes: 8 servings

Preparation: 20 minutes

Cooking: 15 minutes

Ready In: 3 hours 35 minutes

"This is my absolute favorite marinade for chicken. I could eat this every night! The longer you let it marinate, the more intense the flavor. I usually let it sit overnight in the refrigerator, but a few hours will do."

INGREDIENTS

1/4 cup soy sauce

3 tablespoons dry white wine

2 tablespoons lemon juice

2 tablespoons vegetable oil

3/4 teaspoon dried Italian-style seasoning

1 teaspoon grated fresh ginger root

1 clove garlic, crushed

1/4 teaspoon onion powder

1 pinch ground black pepper

8 skinless, boneless chicken breast halves - cut into strips

DIRECTIONS

1. In a large, resealable plastic bag, combine the soy sauce, wine, lemon juice, oil, Italian-style seasoning, ginger, garlic, onion powder, and ground black pepper. Place chicken in the bag. Seal, and let marinate in the refrigerator for at least 3 hours, or overnight.

2. Preheat an outdoor grill for medium-high heat.

3. Thread the chicken onto skewers, and set aside. Pour marinade into a small saucepan, and bring to a boil over high heat.

4. Lightly oil the grill grate. Cook chicken on the prepared grill for approximately 8 minutes per side, basting with the sauce several times. Chicken is done when juices run clear.

Yummy Honey Chicken Kabobs

Submitted by: **Ann Marie Lockwood**

Makes: 12 servings

Preparation: 15 minutes

Cooking: 15 minutes

Ready In: 2 hours 30 minutes

"Honey chicken kabobs with veggies. You can marinate overnight and make these kabobs for an outdoor barbecue as a tasty alternative to the usual barbecue fare! Fresh mushrooms and cherry tomatoes can also be used. (This can also be done in the broiler.)"

INGREDIENTS

1/4 cup vegetable oil

1/3 cup honey

1/3 cup soy sauce

1/4 teaspoon ground black pepper

8 skinless, boneless chicken breast halves - cut into 1 inch cubes

2 cloves garlic

5 small onions, cut into 2 inch pieces

2 red bell peppers, cut into 2 inch pieces

skewers

DIRECTIONS

1. In a large bowl, whisk together oil, honey, soy sauce, and pepper. Before adding chicken, reserve a small amount of marinade to brush onto kabobs while cooking. Place the chicken, garlic, onions and peppers in the bowl, and marinate in the refrigerator at least 2 hours (the longer the better).

2. Preheat the grill for high heat.

3. Drain marinade from the chicken and vegetables, and discard marinade. Thread chicken and vegetables alternately onto the skewers.

4. Lightly oil the grill grate. Place the skewers on the grill. Cook for 12 to 15 minutes, until chicken juices run clear. Turn and brush with reserved marinade frequently.

Chicken and Bacon Shish Kabobs

Submitted by: **Angie**

Makes: 6 servings

Preparation: 25 minutes

Cooking: 20 minutes

Ready In: 1 hour 45 minutes

"Tangy marinated chicken and mushrooms, wrapped in bacon and skewered. Excellent for entertaining and trying something new! These are a must try! (They can also be broiled instead of grilled if low on time.)"

INGREDIENTS

1/4 cup soy sauce

1/4 cup cider vinegar

2 tablespoons honey

2 tablespoons canola oil

10 large mushrooms, cut in half

2 green onions, minced

3 skinless, boneless chicken breast halves - cut into chunks

1/2 pound sliced thick cut bacon, cut in half

1 (8 ounce) can pineapple chunks, drained

skewers

DIRECTIONS

1. In a large bowl, mix the soy sauce, cider vinegar, honey, canola oil, and green onions. Place the mushrooms and chicken into the mixture, and stir to coat. Cover, and marinate in the refrigerator at least 1 hour.

2. Preheat grill for high heat.

3. Wrap the chicken chunks with bacon, and thread onto skewers so that the bacon is secured. Alternate with mushroom halves and pineapple chunks.

4. Lightly oil the grill grate. Arrange skewers on the prepared grill. Cook 15 to 20 minutes, brushing occasionally with remaining soy sauce mixture, until bacon is crisp and chicken juices run clear.

Hawaiian Chicken Kabobs

Submitted by: **Dawn**

Makes: 8 servings
Preparation: 10 minutes
Cooking: 20 minutes
Ready In: 2 hours 30 minutes

"These kabobs are tender, sweet, and delicious. They're easy to make and only require a few ingredients."

INGREDIENTS

3 tablespoons soy sauce

3 tablespoons brown sugar

2 tablespoons sherry

1 tablespoon sesame oil

1/4 teaspoon ground ginger

1/4 teaspoon garlic powder

8 skinless, boneless chicken breast halves - cut into 2 inch pieces

1 (20 ounce) can pineapple chunks, drained

skewers

DIRECTIONS

1. In a shallow glass dish, mix the soy sauce, brown sugar, sherry, sesame oil, ginger, and garlic powder. Stir the chicken pieces and pineapple into the marinade until well coated. Cover, and marinate in the refrigerator at least 2 hours.

2. Preheat grill to medium-high heat.

3. Lightly oil the grill grate. Thread chicken and pineapple alternately onto skewers. Grill 15 to 20 minutes, turning occasionally, or until chicken juices run clear.

Pineapple Chicken Tenders

Submitted by: **Hillary Roberts**

Makes: 10 appetizer servings

Preparation: 30 minutes

Cooking: 10 minutes

Ready In: 1 hour 10 minutes

"Delicious little bites for an appetizer or a light meal with a salad!"

INGREDIENTS

1 cup pineapple juice

1/2 cup packed brown sugar

1/3 cup light soy sauce

2 pounds chicken breast tenderloins or strips

skewers

DIRECTIONS

1. In a small saucepan over medium heat, mix pineapple juice, brown sugar, and soy sauce. Remove from heat just before the mixture comes to a boil.

2. Place chicken tenders in a medium bowl. Cover with the pineapple marinade, and refrigerate for at least 30 minutes.

3. Preheat grill for medium heat. Thread chicken lengthwise onto wooden skewers.

4. Lightly oil the grill grate. Grill chicken tenders 5 minutes per side, or until juices run clear. They cook quickly, so watch them closely.

Chili-Lime Chicken Kabobs

Submitted by: **Simmi Gupta**

Makes: 4 servings

Preparation: 15 minutes

Cooking: 15 minutes

Ready In: 1 hour 30 minutes

"I invented this recipe for a quick dinner. I only marinated the chicken for one hour, but I am sure if you marinate longer, it would taste even better."

INGREDIENTS

3 tablespoons olive oil

1 1/2 tablespoons red wine vinegar

1 lime, juiced

1 teaspoon chili powder

1/2 teaspoon paprika

1/2 teaspoon onion powder

1/2 teaspoon garlic powder

cayenne pepper to taste

salt and freshly ground black pepper to taste

1 pound skinless, boneless chicken breast halves - cut into 1 1/2 inch pieces

skewers

DIRECTIONS

1. In a small bowl, whisk together the olive oil, vinegar, and lime juice. Season with chili powder, paprika, onion powder, garlic powder, cayenne pepper, salt, and black pepper. Place the chicken in a shallow baking dish with the sauce, and stir to coat. Cover, and marinate in the refrigerator at least 1 hour.

2. Preheat the grill for medium-high heat. Thread chicken onto skewers, and discard marinade.

3. Lightly oil the grill grate. Grill skewers for 10 to 15 minutes, or until the chicken juices run clear.

Indonesian Satay

Submitted by: **Estherlita Santoso**

Makes: 6 servings

Preparation: 25 minutes

Cooking: 20 minutes

Ready In: 1 hour

"This is an original Indonesian satay. I send it from a long way. Hope all over the world, readers can enjoy it."

INGREDIENTS

3 tablespoons soy sauce

3 tablespoons tomato sauce

1 tablespoon peanut oil

2 cloves garlic, peeled and minced

1 pinch ground black pepper

1 pinch ground cumin

6 skinless, boneless chicken breast halves - cubed

1 tablespoon vegetable oil

1/4 cup minced onion

1 clove garlic, peeled and minced

1 cup water

1/2 cup chunky peanut butter

2 tablespoons soy sauce

2 tablespoons white sugar

1 tablespoon lemon juice

skewers

DIRECTIONS

1. In a bowl, mix soy sauce, tomato sauce, peanut oil, garlic, black pepper, and cumin. Place chicken into the mixture, and stir to coat. Cover, and marinate in the refrigerator for at least 15 minutes, but not overnight. This will make the meat too dark.

2. Preheat the grill for high heat.

3. Heat vegetable oil in a saucepan over medium heat, and saute onion and garlic until lightly browned. Mix in water, peanut butter, soy sauce, and sugar. Cook and stir until well blended. Remove from heat, mix in lemon juice, and set aside.

4. Lightly oil the grill grate. Thread chicken onto skewers, and discard marinade. Grill skewers about 5 minutes per side, until chicken juices run clear. Serve with the peanut sauce.

Chicken Tikka Masala

Submitted by: **Yakuta**

Makes: 4 servings

Preparation: 30 minutes

Cooking: 50 minutes

Ready In: 2 hours 20 minutes

"This is an easy recipe for Chicken Tikka Masala - Chicken marinated in yogurt and spices and then served in a tomato cream sauce. Serve with rice or warm pita bread."

INGREDIENTS

1 cup yogurt

1 tablespoon lemon juice

2 teaspoons ground cumin

1 teaspoon ground cinnamon

2 teaspoons cayenne pepper

2 teaspoons freshly ground black pepper

1 tablespoon minced fresh ginger

4 teaspoons salt, or to taste

3 boneless skinless chicken breasts, cut into bite-size pieces

4 long skewers

1 tablespoon butter

1 clove garlic, minced

1 jalapeno pepper, finely chopped

2 teaspoons ground cumin

2 teaspoons paprika

3 teaspoons salt, or to taste

1 (8 ounce) can tomato sauce

1 cup heavy cream

1/4 cup chopped fresh cilantro

DIRECTIONS

1. In a large bowl, combine yogurt, lemon juice, 2 teaspoons cumin, cinnamon, cayenne, black pepper, ginger, and 4 teaspoons salt. Stir in chicken, cover, and refrigerate for 1 hour.

2. Preheat a grill for high heat.

3. Lightly oil the grill grate. Thread chicken onto skewers, and discard marinade. Grill until juices run clear, about 5 minutes on each side.

4. Melt butter in a large heavy skillet over medium heat. Saute garlic and jalapeno for 1 minute. Season with 2 teaspoons cumin, paprika, and 3 teaspoons salt. Stir in tomato sauce and cream. Simmer on low heat until sauce thickens, about 20 minutes. Add grilled chicken, and simmer for 10 minutes. Transfer to a serving platter, and garnish with fresh cilantro.

Seasoned Turkey Burgers

Submitted by: **Kym 22**

Makes: 6 servings

Preparation: 10 minutes

Cooking: 20 minutes

Ready In: 40 minutes

"These burgers are great on the 'que' or indoors. Dress them up as you like, even on a whole wheat bun. Baked garlic home fries go great with it! Serve with the 'works': lettuce, tomato, avocado, sprouts, onion, mayonnaise, mustard, ketchup, etc."

INGREDIENTS

1¹/₂ pounds ground turkey breast

1 (1 ounce) package dry onion soup mix

¹/₂ teaspoon ground black pepper

¹/₂ teaspoon garlic powder

1¹/₂ tablespoons soy sauce

1 egg, lightly beaten (optional)

6 hamburger buns, split

DIRECTIONS

1. In a large bowl, mix the turkey with the onion soup mix, pepper, garlic powder, soy sauce, and egg. Refrigerate the mixture for about 10 minutes, then form into 6 patties.

2. Preheat the grill for medium-high heat.

3. Lightly oil the grill grate. Place the patties on the grill. Cook for 20 minutes, turning once, or until well done. The inside of the burgers will look whitish in color when cooked through. Serve on buns.

Turkey Burgers

Submitted by: **Krickett**

Makes: 4 servings

Preparation: 10 minutes

Cooking: 20 minutes

Ready In: 30 minutes

"I love to cook and I'm always trying out new recipes on my family. This was an easy and scrumptious new meal idea! My family loved it. Serve on buns with lettuce, tomatoes, and condiments."

INGREDIENTS

1 pound ground turkey

1 packet dry onion soup mix

1/2 cup water

1/2 teaspoon salt

1/2 teaspoon ground black pepper

DIRECTIONS

1. Preheat a grill for high heat.

2. In a large bowl, combine the ground turkey, soup mix, and water. Season with salt and pepper. Mix lightly using your hands, and form into 4 patties.

3. Lightly oil the grill grate. Grill patties 5 to 10 minutes per side, until well done.

Mushroom Blue Cheese Turkey Burgers

Makes: 4 servings

Preparation: 15 minutes

Cooking: 20 minutes

Ready In: 35 minutes

Submitted by: **Trish**

"These are delicious turkey burgers that my kids even love. I make them more than I make beef patties. You would never know that you are using turkey instead of beef. Fabulous and very easy. Serve on toasted buns."

INGREDIENTS

1 pound ground turkey

8 ounces fresh mushrooms, finely chopped

1 onion, finely chopped

2 tablespoons soy sauce

1/2 teaspoon kosher salt

1/4 teaspoon black pepper

1/4 cup crumbled blue cheese

DIRECTIONS

1. Preheat grill for high heat.

2. In a medium bowl, mix together the ground turkey, mushrooms, onion, and soy sauce. Season with kosher salt and pepper. Form into 4 burger patties.

3. Lightly oil the grill grate. Place patties on the prepared grill, and cook for 10 minutes per side, or until well done. Top with blue cheese during the last few minutes.

Thai Chicken Burgers

Submitted by: **Timothy Johnson**

Makes: 8 servings

Preparation: 15 minutes

Cooking: 15 minutes

Ready In: 1 hour 30 minutes

"Perfect for a more exotic barbecue, these Thai chicken burgers combine ground chicken with sweet, tangy peanut sauce and red chili curry paste. Barbecue or pan-fry, and serve with coconut-mint mayo on toasted rolls."

INGREDIENTS

1 cup mayonnaise

1/4 cup flaked coconut, finely chopped

1 tablespoon chopped fresh mint

2 pounds ground chicken

2 1/2 cups panko bread crumbs

1/2 cup Thai peanut sauce

2 tablespoons red curry paste

2 tablespoons minced green onion

2 tablespoons minced fresh parsley

2 teaspoons soy sauce

3 cloves garlic, minced

2 teaspoons lemon juice

2 teaspoons lime juice

1 tablespoon hot pepper sauce

8 hamburger buns, split and toasted

DIRECTIONS

1. In a small bowl, mix together mayonnaise, coconut, and mint. Cover, and refrigerate for at least 1 hour.

2. In a large bowl, mix together ground chicken, panko crumbs, Thai peanut sauce, curry paste, green onion, parsley, soy sauce, garlic, lemon juice, lime juice, and hot pepper sauce. Be careful not to over-mix. Divide into 8 equal size balls. Flatten into patties about 1/2 inch thick.

3. Preheat the grill for medium-high heat.

4. Lightly oil the grill grate. Grill burgers for 6 to 8 minutes per side, or until well done. Serve on toasted buns with Coconut-Mint Mayonnaise.

Chicken Melt

Submitted by: **Annie**

Makes: 4 servings

Preparation: 15 minutes

Cooking: 25 minutes

Ready In: 40 minutes

"This is a great change from beef! If you like onions and Swiss cheese, you'll LOVE this combination with chicken. Good summer dinner! I serve this with fresh fruit and chips!"

INGREDIENTS

1 tablespoon butter

1 onion, sliced into thin rings

1 teaspoon garlic powder

4 skinless, boneless chicken breasts

1/2 cup red wine

1 teaspoon dried rosemary

1/4 teaspoon dried thyme

4 slices Swiss cheese

4 English muffins, split and toasted

DIRECTIONS

1. Preheat the grill for high heat.

2. Melt the butter in a skillet over medium heat. Place the onion slices in the skillet, sprinkle with garlic powder, and saute until onions are translucent. Remove from heat, and set aside.

3. Lightly oil the grill grate. Place the chicken breast halves on the grill, and sprinkle with wine, rosemary, and thyme. Cook for about 8 minutes. Turn, and continue cooking 8 minutes, or until juices run clear. Place a slice of cheese on each breast half, and top with onions. Cook until cheese starts to melt. Serve on toasted English muffins.

Grilled Chicken Quesadillas

Submitted by: **Thuy Ortiz**

Makes: 6 servings

Preparation: 35 minutes

Cooking: 30 minutes

Ready In: 1 hour 20 minutes

"This delicious recipe is prepared by using adobo seasoned grilled boneless chicken thighs, layering tortillas with a combination of the chicken, cheese, and onion, and heating directly on the grill. Serve with salsa and sour cream."

INGREDIENTS

2 pounds boneless, skinless chicken thighs

adobo seasoning to taste

12 (10 inch) flour tortillas

1 1/2 cups shredded Mexican cheese blend

1 onion, chopped

1 (6 ounce) can sliced black olives, drained

1 (7 ounce) can diced green chilies, drained

DIRECTIONS

1. Place the chicken on a plate, and sprinkle with adobo seasoning on both sides. Let it marinate for 15 minutes.

2. Heat grill for medium-high heat.

3. Lightly oil the grill grate. Place chicken on grill, and cook for 10 minutes per side, or until juices run clear. Remove chicken from grill, and cut into bite-size pieces.

4. Place one or two tortillas on the grill, and sprinkle with a thin layer of cheese, chicken, onion, olives, and chilies. Top with another tortilla, and grill until brown and crispy on both sides, about 3 minutes per side. Repeat with remaining ingredients. Cut into wedges to serve.

Grilled Chicken and Pasta Salad

Makes: 4 servings

Preparation: 15 minutes

Cooking: 30 minutes

Ready In: 45 minutes

Submitted by: **Ann Marie Lockwood**

"This salad is very filling and is used as a meal in my home. Everyone always loves it! It is also quick and easy. Note: I have also added olives, hard boiled eggs, and red bell pepper to this salad. Enjoy with your favorite dressing!"

INGREDIENTS

4 skinless, boneless chicken breast halves

steak seasoning to taste

8 ounces rotini pasta

8 ounces mozzarella cheese, cubed

1 red onion, chopped

1 head romaine lettuce, chopped

6 cherry tomatoes, chopped

DIRECTIONS

1. Preheat the grill for high heat. Season both sides of chicken breast halves with steak seasoning.

2. Lightly oil the grill grate. Grill chicken 6 to 8 minutes per side, or until juices run clear. Remove from heat, cool, and cut into strips.

3. Meanwhile, place the rotini pasta in a large pot of lightly salted boiling water. Cook 8 to 10 minutes, until al dente. Drain, and rinse with cold water to cool.

4. In a large bowl, mix together the cheese, onion, lettuce, and tomatoes. Toss with the cooled chicken and pasta to serve.

BBQ Chicken Salad

Submitted by: **Deborah Noe**

Makes: 4 servings

Preparation: 15 minutes

Cooking: 20 minutes

Ready In: 50 minutes

"This is a great way to use up grilled chicken leftovers. Serve on a bed of greens."

INGREDIENTS

2 skinless, boneless chicken breast halves

4 stalks celery, chopped

1 large red bell pepper, diced

1/2 red onion, diced

1 (8.75 ounce) can sweet corn, drained

1/4 cup barbeque sauce

2 tablespoons fat-free mayonnaise

DIRECTIONS

1. Preheat grill for high heat.

2. Lightly oil grate. Grill chicken 10 minutes on each side, or until juices run clear. Remove from heat, cool, and cube.

3. In a large bowl, toss together the chicken, celery, red bell pepper, onion, and corn.

4. In a small bowl, mix together the barbeque sauce and mayonnaise. Pour over the chicken and veggies. Stir, and chill until ready to serve.

Grilled Orange Vinaigrette Chicken Salad

Makes: 6 servings

Preparation: 15 minutes

Cooking: 20 minutes

Ready In: 35 minutes

Submitted by: **Jill**

"This is a tasty and cool salad that is perfect for a summer supper. If you don't like broccoli and carrots, substitute your favorite fresh vegetables!"

INGREDIENTS

½ cup orange juice

½ cup white wine vinegar

¼ cup olive oil

4 tablespoons salt-free garlic and herb seasoning blend

1½ tablespoons white sugar

1 pound skinless, boneless chicken breast halves

1 head romaine lettuce- rinsed, dried and chopped

1 (11 ounce) can mandarin oranges, drained

1 cup chopped fresh broccoli

1 cup chopped baby carrots

DIRECTIONS

1. Preheat grill for medium-high heat.

2. In a bowl, whisk together the orange juice, vinegar, olive oil, seasoning blend, and sugar. Set aside about ½ cup for basting.

3. Lightly oil the grill grate. Grill chicken for 6 to 8 minutes on each side, basting frequently with the reserved portion of the dressing, or until juices run clear. Cool, and cut into strips. Discard basting sauce.

4. In a large bowl, toss together the lettuce, oranges, broccoli, and carrots. Top the salad with grilled chicken strips, and drizzle with remaining dressing to serve.

Chicken Berry Salad

Submitted by: **Katie Mines**

Makes: 6 servings

Preparation: 20 minutes

Cooking: 15 minutes

Ready In: 35 minutes

"This recipe uses three kinds of fresh berries and your choice of mixed salad greens, all tossed together with grilled chicken and a special honey mustard dressing. This is my favorite summer salad - I make it for company all the time! And it is very pretty!"

INGREDIENTS

1 (.75 ounce) packet honey mustard salad dressing mix

1/4 cup cider vinegar

1/2 cup vegetable oil

2 tablespoons orange juice

1 pound skinless, boneless chicken breast halves

8 cups mixed salad greens

1 cup sliced fresh strawberries

1/2 cup fresh blueberries

1/2 cup fresh raspberries

8 ounces sugar snap peas

1/2 cup toasted pecans

DIRECTIONS

1. In a medium bowl, prepare the dressing according to package directions, using vinegar and oil, and substituting orange juice for the water; set aside.

2. Preheat the grill for high heat.

3. Lightly oil the grill grate. Grill the chicken 6 to 8 minutes on each side, or until juices run clear. Remove from heat, cool, and slice into strips.

4. In a large bowl, toss together the chicken, salad greens, strawberries, blueberries, raspberries, peas, and pecans. Pour in the prepared dressing, and toss to coat.

Caribbean Chicken Salad

Submitted by: **Marcy Dzurisin**

Makes: 4 servings

Preparation: 30 minutes

Cooking: 15 minutes

Ready In: 2 hours 45 minutes

"With just a few things done ahead of time, your dinner can be a breeze."

INGREDIENTS

2 skinless, boneless chicken breast halves

1/2 cup teriyaki marinade sauce

2 tomatoes, seeded and chopped

1/2 cup chopped onion

2 teaspoons minced jalapeno pepper

2 teaspoons chopped fresh cilantro

1/4 cup Dijon mustard

1/4 cup honey

1 1/2 tablespoons white sugar

1 tablespoon vegetable oil

1 1/2 tablespoons cider vinegar

1 1/2 teaspoons lime juice

3/4 pound mixed salad greens

1 (8 ounce) can pineapple chunks, drained

4 cups corn tortilla chips

DIRECTIONS

1. Place the chicken in a bowl, and cover with the teriyaki marinade sauce. Marinate at least 2 hours in the refrigerator.

2. In a small bowl mix the tomatoes, onion, jalapeno pepper, and cilantro. Cover salsa, and refrigerate.

3. In a small bowl, mix the mustard, honey, sugar, oil, vinegar, and lime juice. Cover dressing, and refrigerate.

4. Preheat the grill for high heat.

5. Lightly oil grill grate. Place chicken on the grill, and discard marinade. Cook for 6 to 8 minutes on each side, or until juices run clear.

6. Arrange mixed salad greens on plates. Spoon some of the salsa over each salad, and sprinkle with 1/4 of the pineapple chunks. Break tortilla chips into large chunks, and sprinkle over salads. Lay some of the grilled chicken strips on each salad. Finally, drizzle dressing over each salad, and serve.

Accidental Grilled Chicken Salad

Submitted by: **Karen**

Makes: 6 servings
Preparation: 15 minutes
Cooking: 30 minutes
Ready In: 2 hours

"Was expecting a few hungry friends to walk in as I started cooking, but they called and had an emergency. Fortunately nothing bad, but there I was with too much food. Chopped everything up, added mayo, and a generous slurp of hot sauce (the way I like it). Not your run-of-the-mill chicken salad. Good way to finish up those leftovers! I put the onion slices and mushrooms in a grill basket so they could be turned without falling apart as they cooked.
Hope you like it!"

INGREDIENTS

4 boneless, skinless chicken breast halves

2 tablespoons lemon juice

2 tablespoons olive oil

2 teaspoons lemon pepper

2 Vidalia onions, thickly sliced

4 large mushroom caps, chopped

1 cup mayonnaise

hot sauce to taste (optional)

salt and pepper to taste

DIRECTIONS

1. Place chicken breast halves in a large resealable plastic bag with lemon juice, olive oil, and lemon pepper. Shake to coat, and marinate in the refrigerator for at least 1 hour.

2. Preheat a grill for high heat.

3. Lightly oil the grill grate. Place the Vidalia onions and mushrooms on the grill, and cook until lightly charred on both sides; set aside. Place chicken onto the grill, and discard marinade. Cook for 15 minutes, turning once, or until juices run clear. Remove from heat, cool, and chop.

4. In a large bowl, thoroughly mix the onions, mushrooms, chicken, and mayonnaise. Season with hot sauce, salt, and pepper. Cover, and refrigerate until serving.

seafood

Putting fish over fire can be tricky, as its fragile flesh can easily dry out or fall apart. But when it all goes swimmingly, oh how succulent that seafood can be! High-fat and firm-fleshed fishes like salmon, halibut, and tuna were just made for the grill. Oil the grate well, leave the skin on when possible, and watch it to make sure it doesn't overcook; your vigilance will be rewarded with a meal to remember.

Lemon Ginger Shrimp

Submitted by: **Zuzka**

Makes: 9 servings

Preparation: 20 minutes

Cooking: 6 minutes

Ready In: 2 hours 30 minutes

"Barbequed shrimp marinated in lemon and ginger with a hint of sesame."

INGREDIENTS

3 pounds jumbo shrimp, peeled and deveined

1/2 cup olive oil

2 teaspoons sesame oil

1/4 cup lemon juice

1 onion, chopped

2 cloves garlic, peeled

2 tablespoons grated fresh ginger root

2 tablespoons minced fresh cilantro leaves

1 teaspoon paprika

1/2 teaspoon salt

1/2 teaspoon ground black pepper

skewers

DIRECTIONS

1. In a blender or food processor, process the olive oil, sesame oil, lemon juice, onion, garlic, ginger, cilantro, paprika, salt, and pepper until smooth. Reserve a small amount for basting. Pour the remaining mixture into a dish, add shrimp, and stir to coat. Cover, and refrigerate for 2 hours.

2. Preheat grill for medium heat. Thread shrimp onto skewers, piercing once near the tail and once near the head. Discard marinade.

3. Lightly oil grill grate. Grill shrimp for 2 to 3 minutes per side, or until opaque. Baste with reserved sauce while cooking.

Big M's Spicy Lime Grilled Prawns

Submitted by: **Marcus Hender**

Makes: 12 servings

Preparation: 30 minutes

Cooking: 5 minutes

Ready In: 4 hours 35 minutes

"Succulent and moist grilled prawns. Serve with salad, potatoes, and bread. Enjoy!"

INGREDIENTS

48 large tiger prawns, peeled and deveined

4 limes, zested and juiced

4 green chile peppers, seeded and chopped

4 cloves garlic, crushed

1 (2 inch) piece fresh ginger root, chopped

1 medium onion, coarsely chopped

skewers

DIRECTIONS

1. Place the prawns and lime zest in a large, non-metallic bowl. Place the lime juice, chile pepper, garlic, ginger, and onion in a food processor or blender, and process until smooth. You may need to add a little oil to facilitate blending. Pour over the bowl of prawns, and stir to coat. Cover, and refrigerate for 4 hours.

2. Preheat grill for medium-high heat. Thread prawns onto skewers, piercing each first through the tail, and then the head.

3. Brush grill grate with oil. Cook prawns for 5 minutes, turning once, or until opaque.

Spicy Grilled Shrimp

Submitted by: **Suz**

Makes: 6 servings

Preparation: 15 minutes

Cooking: 6 minutes

Ready In: 21 minutes

"So fast and easy to prepare, these shrimp are destined to be the hit of any barbeque. And, weather not permitting, they work great under the broiler, too."

INGREDIENTS

1 large clove garlic

1 tablespoon coarse salt

1/2 teaspoon cayenne pepper

1 teaspoon paprika

2 tablespoons olive oil

2 teaspoons lemon juice

2 pounds large shrimp, peeled and deveined

8 wedges lemon, for garnish

DIRECTIONS

1. Preheat grill for medium heat.

2. In a small bowl, crush the garlic with the salt. Mix in cayenne pepper and paprika, and then stir in olive oil and lemon juice to form a paste. In a large bowl, toss shrimp with garlic paste until evenly coated.

3. Lightly oil grill grate. Cook shrimp for 2 to 3 minutes per side, or until opaque. Transfer to a serving dish, garnish with lemon wedges, and serve.

Grilled Shrimp Scampi

Submitted by: **Holly Murphy**

Makes: 6 servings

Preparation: 30 minutes

Cooking: 6 minutes

Ready In: 1 hour 6 minutes

"Shrimp marinated in lemon, garlic, and parsley for 30 minutes, then grilled. Can be used as an appetizer or main dish. This recipe also works well with scallops."

INGREDIENTS

1/4 cup olive oil

1/4 cup lemon juice

3 tablespoons chopped fresh parsley

1 tablespoon minced garlic

ground black pepper to taste

crushed red pepper flakes to taste (optional)

1 1/2 pounds medium shrimp, peeled and deveined

DIRECTIONS

1. In a large, non-reactive bowl, stir together the olive oil, lemon juice, parsley, garlic, and black pepper. Season with crushed red pepper, if desired. Add shrimp, and toss to coat. Marinate in the refrigerator for 30 minutes.

2. Preheat grill for high heat. Thread shrimp onto skewers, piercing once near the tail and once near the head. Discard any remaining marinade.

3. Lightly oil grill grate. Grill for 2 to 3 minutes per side, or until opaque.

Grilled Marinated Shrimp

Submitted by: **Robbie Rice**

Makes: 6 servings

Preparation: 30 minutes

Cooking: 10 minutes

Ready In: 2 hours 40 minutes

"This makes the best shrimp! Remove from skewers and serve on a bed of pasta with sauce for a great meal."

INGREDIENTS

1 cup olive oil

1/4 cup chopped fresh parsley

1 lemon, juiced

2 tablespoons hot pepper sauce

3 cloves garlic, minced

1 tablespoon tomato paste

2 teaspoons dried oregano

1 teaspoon salt

1 teaspoon ground black pepper

2 pounds large shrimp, peeled and deveined with tails attached

skewers

DIRECTIONS

1. In a mixing bowl, mix together olive oil, parsley, lemon juice, hot sauce, garlic, tomato paste, oregano, salt, and black pepper. Reserve a small amount for basting later. Pour remaining marinade into a large resealable plastic bag with shrimp. Seal, and marinate in the refrigerator for 2 hours.

2. Preheat grill for medium-low heat. Thread shrimp onto skewers, piercing once near the tail and once near the head. Discard marinade.

3. Lightly oil grill grate. Cook shrimp for 5 minutes per side, or until opaque, basting frequently with reserved marinade.

Garlicky Appetizer Shrimp Scampi

Submitted by: **Holly**

Makes: 6 servings

Preparation: 15 minutes

Cooking: 6 minutes

Ready In: 21 minutes

"Quick, garlicky, and delicious shrimp scampi."

INGREDIENTS

6 tablespoons unsalted butter, softened

1/4 cup olive oil

1 tablespoon minced garlic

1 tablespoon minced shallots

2 tablespoons minced fresh chives

salt and freshly ground black pepper to taste

1/2 teaspoon paprika

2 pounds large shrimp - peeled and deveined

DIRECTIONS

1. Preheat grill for high heat.

2. In a large bowl, mix together softened butter, olive oil, garlic, shallots, chives, salt, pepper, and paprika; add the shrimp, and toss to coat.

3. Lightly oil grill grate. Cook the shrimp as close to the flame as possible for 2 to 3 minutes per side, or until opaque.

Marinated Grilled Shrimp

Submitted by: **Rachel**

Makes: 6 servings

Preparation: 15 minutes

Cooking: 6 minutes

Ready In: 55 minutes

"A very simple and easy marinade that makes your shrimp so yummy you don't even need cocktail sauce! Don't let the cayenne pepper scare you, you don't even taste it. My 2 and 4 year-olds love it and eat more shrimp than their parents!!! It is also a big hit with company, and easy to prepare. I make this with frozen or fresh shrimp and use my indoor electric grill if the weather is not good for outside grilling. Try it with a salad, baked potato, and garlic bread. You will not be disappointed!!!"

INGREDIENTS

3 cloves garlic, minced

1/3 cup olive oil

1/4 cup tomato sauce

2 tablespoons red wine vinegar

2 tablespoons chopped fresh basil

1/2 teaspoon salt

1/4 teaspoon cayenne pepper

2 pounds fresh shrimp, peeled and deveined

skewers

DIRECTIONS

1. In a large bowl, stir together the garlic, olive oil, tomato sauce, and red wine vinegar. Season with basil, salt, and cayenne pepper. Add shrimp to the bowl, and stir until evenly coated. Cover, and refrigerate for 30 minutes to 1 hour, stirring once or twice.

2. Preheat grill for medium heat. Thread shrimp onto skewers, piercing once near the tail and once near the head. Discard marinade.

3. Lightly oil grill grate. Cook shrimp on preheated grill for 2 to 3 minutes per side, or until opaque.

Honey Grilled Shrimp

Submitted by: **Kendra**

Makes: 3 servings

Preparation: 30 minutes

Cooking: 6 minutes

Ready In: 1 hour 36 minutes

"Easy and delicious! Onions, peppers, and mushrooms are perfect when alternated with shrimp on the skewers. Just cut into bite-sized pieces and add them to the marinade with the shrimp."

INGREDIENTS

1/2 teaspoon garlic powder

1/4 tablespoon ground black pepper

1/3 cup Worcestershire sauce

2 tablespoons dry white wine

2 tablespoons Italian-style salad dressing

1 pound large shrimp, peeled and deveined with tails attached

1/4 cup honey

1/4 cup butter, melted

2 tablespoons Worcestershire sauce

skewers

DIRECTIONS

1. In a large bowl, mix together garlic powder, black pepper, 1/3 cup Worcestershire sauce, wine, and salad dressing; add shrimp, and toss to coat. Cover, and marinate in the refrigerator for 1 hour.

2. Preheat grill for high heat. Thread shrimp onto skewers, piercing once near the tail and once near the head. Discard marinade.

3. In a small bowl, stir together honey, melted butter, and remaining 2 tablespoons Worcestershire sauce. Set aside for basting.

4. Lightly oil grill grate. Grill shrimp for 2 to 3 minutes per side, or until opaque. Baste occasionally with the honey-butter sauce while grilling.

Basil Shrimp

Submitted by: **Gail Laulette**

Makes: 9 servings

Preparation: 25 minutes

Cooking: 5 minutes

Ready In: 1 hour 30 minutes

"This was given to me by my friend, Elaine. It is one of the most delicious shrimp recipes for the BBQ I have ever had, and it is so easy. My son would eat the whole recipe if I didn't watch him."

INGREDIENTS

2¹/₂ tablespoons olive oil

¹/₄ cup butter, melted

1¹/₂ lemons, juiced

3 tablespoons brown mustard

4 ounces minced fresh basil

3 cloves garlic, minced

salt to taste

white pepper

3 pounds fresh shrimp, peeled and deveined

skewers

DIRECTIONS

1. In a shallow, non-porous dish or bowl, mix together olive oil and melted butter. Stir in lemon juice, mustard, basil, and garlic, and season with salt and white pepper. Add shrimp, and toss to coat. Cover, and refrigerate for 1 hour.

2. Preheat grill to high heat. Remove shrimp from marinade, and thread onto skewers. Discard marinade.

3. Lightly oil grill grate, and arrange skewers on preheated grill. Cook for 4 minutes, turning once, or until opaque.

Hawaiian Shrimp

Submitted by: **Mina**

Makes: 6 servings

Preparation: 30 minutes

Cooking: 8 minutes

Ready In: 38 minutes

"Pineapple and shrimp, basted with a sweet and sour sauce, lends a tropical touch to any BBQ. This is a favorite!"

INGREDIENTS

2 pounds medium shrimp, peeled and deveined

2 (20 ounce) cans pineapple chunks, juice reserved

1/2 pound bacon slices, cut into 2 inch pieces

2 large red bell peppers, chopped

1/2 pound fresh mushrooms, stems removed

2 cups cherry tomatoes

1 cup sweet and sour sauce

skewers

DIRECTIONS

1. Preheat grill for high heat.

2. Thread shrimp, pineapple, bacon, red bell peppers, mushroom caps, and cherry tomatoes on skewers, alternating ingredients. Place in a shallow baking dish. In a small bowl, mix sweet and sour sauce with reserved pineapple juice. Reserve a small amount for basting. Pour remaining sauce over skewers.

3. Lightly oil grill grate. Cook kabobs on preheated grill for 6 to 8 minutes, or until opaque, basting often with reserved sauce.

Dad's Excellent Scallops

Submitted by: **Donna Francis**

Makes: 8 servings

Preparation: 20 minutes

Cooking: 13 minutes

Ready In: 33 minutes

"Large sea scallops wrapped in prosciutto, basted with butter, and grilled. Serve with your favorite dipping sauce - ketchup, tartar, or cocktail sauce are all great with these."

INGREDIENTS

2 pounds shelled, large sea scallops

1/2 pound prosciutto, thinly sliced

1/2 cup butter, melted

toothpicks, soaked in water

DIRECTIONS

1. Preheat grill for medium-high heat.

2. Wrap each scallop with a thin slice of prosciutto, and secure with a toothpick.

3. Lightly oil grill grate. Arrange scallops on the grill, and baste with butter. Cook for 5 minutes, turn, and baste with butter. Cook for another 8 minutes, or until opaque.

Crab Stuffed Lobster Rayna

Submitted by: **Rayna Jordan**

Makes: 4 servings

Preparation: 20 minutes

Cooking: 27 minutes

Ready In: 47 minutes

"To die for! I serve these to company on special occasions with warm garlic and lemon butter. My guests are still talking about the first time I whipped these up over five years ago!"

INGREDIENTS

4 (6 ounce) shelled raw lobster tails

1 tablespoon butter

1 tablespoon minced celery

1 green onion, minced

1½ teaspoons all-purpose flour

⅛ teaspoon dry mustard

⅛ teaspoon cayenne pepper

⅓ cup cold milk

1 (6 ounce) can crabmeat, drained and flaked

2 tablespoons dry bread crumbs

DIRECTIONS

1. Preheat grill for medium heat.

2. Butterfly the lobster tails by carefully cutting a slit down the top side, without cutting all the way through to the bottom. Flip the tail over, and carefully cut the shiny membrane without cutting the meat on the underside. This will prevent the tails from curling as they cook. Set tails aside.

3. In a skillet, melt the butter over medium heat. Cook and stir the celery and green onion in butter until tender. Stir in the flour, dry mustard, and cayenne pepper. Using a wire whisk, mix in cold milk slowly, whisking constantly to prevent lumps from forming. Continue cooking, stirring occasionally, until thickened. Remove from heat. Stir in crab meat and bread crumbs. Spoon crab mixture into lobster tails.

4. Arrange tails on the preheated grill, and close the lid. Cook for 12 minutes, or until lobster meat is opaque and the crab mixture is heated through.

Grilled Rock Lobster Tails

Submitted by: **Joe Nekrasz**

Makes: 2 servings

Preparation: 15 minutes

Cooking: 12 minutes

Ready In: 27 minutes

"Grilled rock lobster tails lightly seasoned with lemon and garlic. Ready in no time at all, and oh so delicious!"

INGREDIENTS

1 tablespoon lemon juice

1/2 cup olive oil

1 teaspoon salt

1 teaspoon paprika

1/8 teaspoon white pepper

1/8 teaspoon garlic powder

2 (10 ounce) rock lobster tails

DIRECTIONS

1. Preheat grill for high heat.

2. Squeeze lemon juice into a small bowl, and slowly whisk in olive oil. Whisk in salt, paprika, white pepper, and garlic powder. Split lobster tails lengthwise with a large knife, and brush flesh side of tail with marinade.

3. Lightly oil grill grate. Place tails, flesh side down, on preheated grill. Cook for 10 to 12 minutes, turning once, and basting frequently with marinade. Discard any remaining marinade. Lobster is done when opaque and firm to the touch.

Alaskan BBQ Salmon

Submitted by: **Tim Jannott**

Makes: 16 servings

Preparation: 10 minutes

Cooking: 17 minutes

Ready In: 27 minutes

"Simple and sweet, this recipe for grilling a whole salmon fillet is sure to be a family favorite."

INGREDIENTS

1 cup brown sugar

1/2 cup honey

1 dash liquid smoke flavoring

1/2 cup apple cider vinegar

1 (4 pound) whole salmon fillet

DIRECTIONS

1. Preheat grill for high heat.

2. In a small bowl, mix together brown sugar, honey, liquid smoke, and vinegar.

3. Brush one side of the salmon with the basting sauce. Place the salmon on the grill, basted side down. After about 7 minutes, generously baste the top, and turn over. Cook for about 8 more minutes, then brush on more basting sauce, turn, and cook for 2 minutes. Take care not to overcook the salmon as it will lose its juices and flavor if cooked too long.

Alder Plank Smoked Salmon

Submitted by: **Smokin' Ron**

Makes: 12 servings

Preparation: 15 minutes

Cooking: 6 hours

Ready In: 10 hours 15 minutes

"This smoked salmon derives its flavor from Alder wood planks. I get these planks at the local lumber yard. Be sure you tell whoever helps you that you are cooking salmon on the wood so that you do not get any creosote wood or other treated wood. Also, make sure you know what plank size will fit in your smoker before you go to get the wood. This salmon will come out very moist and smoky, so be prepared for some of the best smoked fish you've ever eaten!"

INGREDIENTS

Basic Brine (page 51)

1 (3 pound) salmon fillet

alder wood plank

freshly ground black pepper to taste

2 tablespoons packed brown sugar

1 tablespoon water

DIRECTIONS

1. Soak the salmon fillet in a brine solution for at least 4 hours, but preferably overnight. Also, submerge the alder wood plank in water, placing a heavy object on top of it to prevent floating

2. Preheat an outdoor smoker for 160 to 180°F (70 to 80°C).

3. Remove the salmon from the brine, rinse thoroughly under cold running water, and pat dry with paper towels. Remove the wood plank from the water, and lay the fish out on the plank. Season with freshly ground black pepper.

4. Smoke the salmon for at least 2 hours, checking after 1½ hours for doneness. The fish is done when it flakes with a fork, but it should also not be too salty. As the fish smokes, the salt content reduces. Adjust the cooking time and salty flavor to your taste. (Note: Smoking a fillet can take 2 to 6 hours depending on your taste, the size of the fillet, and the fat content of the fish.)

5. During the last 30 minutes of smoking, mix together the brown sugar and water to form a paste. Brush this liberally onto the salmon.

Grilled Salmon I

Submitted by: **Tina**

Makes: 6 servings

Preparation: 15 minutes

Cooking: 16 minutes

Ready In: 2 hours 31 minutes

"A simple soy sauce and brown sugar marinade, with hints of lemon and garlic, are the perfect salty-sweet complement to rich salmon fillets. Even my 9 year old loves this recipe!"

INGREDIENTS

1½ pounds salmon fillets

lemon pepper to taste

garlic powder to taste

salt to taste

⅓ cup soy sauce

⅓ cup brown sugar

⅓ cup water

¼ cup vegetable oil

DIRECTIONS

1. Season salmon fillets with lemon pepper, garlic powder, and salt.

2. In a small bowl, stir together soy sauce, brown sugar, water, and vegetable oil until sugar is dissolved. Place fish in a large resealable plastic bag with the soy sauce mixture, seal, and turn to coat. Refrigerate for at least 2 hours.

3. Preheat grill for medium heat.

4. Lightly oil grill grate. Place salmon on the preheated grill, and discard marinade. Cook salmon for 6 to 8 minutes per side, or until the fish flakes easily with a fork.

Morgan's Grilled Fish

Submitted by: **Morgan**

Makes: 4 servings

Preparation: 10 minutes

Cooking: 10 minutes

Ready In: 50 minutes

"A great summertime recipe for grilled salmon fillets. An herb and lemon marinade makes for a wonderfully light and flavorful preparation. Grilled onions would be an excellent addition!"

INGREDIENTS

¼ cup olive oil

1 tablespoon dried parsley

2 tablespoons dried thyme

1 tablespoon dried rosemary

1 clove garlic, minced

4 (6 ounce) fillets salmon

1 lemon, juiced

DIRECTIONS

1. Preheat grill for medium heat.

2. In a shallow glass dish, mix the olive oil, parsley, thyme, rosemary, and garlic. Place the salmon in the dish, turning coat. Squeeze lemon juice over each fillet. Cover, and marinate in the refrigerator for 30 minutes.

3. Lightly oil grill grate. Transfer salmon to the grill, and discard any remaining marinade. Cook salmon on preheated grill over medium heat for 8 to 10 minutes, turning once. Fish is done when it flakes easily with a fork.

Profanity Salmon

Submitted by: **Heather**

Makes: 4 servings

Preparation: 30 minutes

Cooking: 15 minutes

Ready In: 45 minutes

"This is some darn good salmon! And believe me it is easy too. This is also one of those recipes that you can have fun with. Season to your tastes, use more or less ingredients, make it your own. Whenever there is a summer BBQ this is what I make (because even I can't mess up on it)."

INGREDIENTS

½ cup mayonnaise

3 tablespoons teriyaki sauce

¼ teaspoon wasabi paste, or to taste

1 (1 1/2 pound) salmon fillet

salt and pepper to taste

1 green bell pepper, sliced

1 onion, finely chopped

DIRECTIONS

1. Preheat grill for high heat.

2. In a small bowl, blend mayonnaise, teriyaki sauce, and wasabi paste. Place salmon on a large piece of aluminum foil. Spread the mayonnaise mixture over the top of the fillet. Top with green pepper and onion. Season with salt and pepper. Fold the foil around the food and seal into a packet.

3. Place fish on the preheated grill. Cook for 10 to 15 minutes, or until the fish is easily flaked with a fork.

Salmon Tango

Submitted by: **Hilda**

Makes: 5 servings

Preparation: 15 minutes

Cooking: 8 minutes

Ready In: 1 hour 23 minutes

"This rich and delicious sweet and sour marinade is simply wonderful with grilled salmon, and quite easy to prepare!"

INGREDIENTS

1/4 cup butter, melted

1/4 cup brown sugar

1 tablespoon soy sauce

2 tablespoons lemon juice

2 tablespoons white wine

1 1/4 pounds salmon fillets

DIRECTIONS

1. In a medium glass bowl, mix together the melted butter, brown sugar, soy sauce, lemon juice, and white wine. Stir until brown sugar has dissolved. Reserve a small amount to use as a basting sauce; the remainder is used as a marinade.

2. Place salmon fillets in a large resealable plastic bag. Pour in marinade, seal, and turn to coat salmon. Refrigerate at least 1 hour, turning once.

3. Preheat grill for medium-high heat.

4. Lightly oil grill grate. Place salmon on grill, and discard marinade. Cook salmon for 3 to 4 minutes per side, or until easily flaked with a fork. Baste with reserved sauce while grilling.

Grilled Salmon with Habanero-Lime Butter

Submitted by: **Mike Smith**

Makes: 4 servings

Preparation: 25 minutes

Cooking: 16 minutes

Ready In: 2 hours 41 minutes

"Grilled salmon marinated in orange juice, lime juice, tequila, and habanero peppers, then served with a habanero-lime butter. Remove the seeds from the peppers to tame the heat. You may wish to wear rubber gloves while chopping peppers to protect your hands from the spicy oils."

INGREDIENTS

1/4 cup vegetable oil

1/2 cup orange juice

3 tablespoons lime juice

1 tablespoon tequila

1 tablespoon grated lime zest

1 tablespoon minced habanero pepper

1 clove garlic, minced

4 (5 ounce) salmon steaks

1/4 cup butter, softened

1/4 teaspoon garlic salt

1 tablespoon lime juice

2 teaspoons minced habanero pepper

2 teaspoons grated lime zest

DIRECTIONS

1. In a bowl, stir together vegetable oil, orange juice, 3 tablespoons lime juice, tequila, 1 tablespoon lime zest, 1 tablespoon habanero pepper, and garlic. Reserve a small amount to use as a basting sauce, and pour the remainder into a shallow baking dish. Place the salmon in the shallow dish, and turn to coat. Cover, and refrigerate for 2 to 4 hours, turning frequently.

2. In a small bowl, mix together softened butter, garlic salt, 1 tablespoon lime juice, 2 teaspoons habanero pepper, and 2 teaspoons lime zest. Cover, and refrigerate.

3. Preheat grill for medium heat.

4. Lightly oil grill grate, and place salmon on the grill. Cook salmon for 5 to 8 minutes per side, or until the fish can be easily flaked with a fork. Transfer to a serving dish, top with habanero butter, and serve.

BBQ Salmon over Mixed Greens

Submitted by: **Holly**

Makes: 6 servings

Preparation: 30 minutes

Cooking: 10 minutes

Ready In: 6 hours 40 minutes

"Barbecued salmon fillets served with a homemade vinaigrette dressing on a bed of mixed greens. This recipe is full of flavor and color and is sure to impress."

INGREDIENTS

2 tablespoons chili powder

1 tablespoon garlic powder

1 tablespoon onion powder

3 tablespoons white sugar

1 tablespoon salt

1/2 teaspoon ground allspice

1/2 teaspoon ground cumin

1/4 teaspoon ground white pepper

1 tablespoon paprika

6 (6 ounce) fillets salmon

olive oil

1 1/2 cups tomato-vegetable juice cocktail

1 tablespoon balsamic or cider vinegar

1/2 cup chopped tomatoes

4 tablespoons olive oil

1 pound mixed salad greens, rinsed and dried

DIRECTIONS

1. In a small bowl, mix together chili powder, garlic powder, onion powder, sugar, salt, allspice, cumin, white pepper, and paprika. Reserve 1 1/2 tablespoons of the mixture for the vinaigrette, and sprinkle remaining spice mixture over salmon fillets. Cover, and refrigerate for 6 hours.

2. Preheat grill for high heat.

3. Lightly oil grill grate, and spread a small amount of olive oil on salmon fillets. Cook salmon 4 to 5 minutes per side, or until easily flaked with a fork.

4. In a small bowl, mix together tomato-vegetable juice cocktail, vinegar, tomatoes, olive oil, and reserved spice mixture to make vinaigrette. Place salad greens in a large bowl, drizzle with vinaigrette, and toss to coat.

5. Divide greens among individual serving plates. Top each plate with a salmon fillet, and spoon any remaining vinaigrette over the salmon.

Grilled Tuna Teriyaki

Submitted by: **Maridele**

Makes: 4 servings

Preparation: 15 minutes

Cooking: 12 minutes

Ready In: 57 minutes

"Delicious right off the grill! Take care not to overcook the steaks, as tuna can quickly become quite dry."

INGREDIENTS

2 tablespoons light soy sauce

1 tablespoon Chinese rice wine

1 large clove garlic, minced

1 tablespoon minced fresh ginger root

4 (6 ounce) tuna steaks (about 3/4 inch thick)

1 tablespoon vegetable oil

DIRECTIONS

1. In a shallow dish, stir together soy sauce, rice wine, garlic, and ginger. Place tuna in the marinade, and turn to coat. Cover, and refrigerate for at least 30 minutes.

2. Preheat grill for medium-high heat.

3. Remove tuna from marinade, and discard remaining liquid. Brush both sides of steaks with oil.

4. Cook tuna for approximately for 3 to 6 minutes per side, or to desired doneness.

Grilled Fish Steaks

Submitted by: **Kimber**

Makes: 8 servings

Preparation: 15 minutes

Cooking: 12 minutes

Ready In: 1 hour 27 minutes

"Very easy, but oh so good! This recipe will work with just about any kind of fish steak."

INGREDIENTS

8 (3 ounce) fillets fresh tuna steaks, 1 inch thick

1/2 cup soy sauce

1/3 cup sherry

1/4 cup vegetable oil

1 tablespoon fresh lime juice

1 clove garlic, minced

DIRECTIONS

1. Place tuna steaks in a shallow baking dish. In a medium bowl, mix soy sauce, sherry, vegetable oil, fresh lime juice, and garlic. Pour the soy sauce mixture over the tuna steaks, and turn to coat. Cover, and refrigerate for at least one hour.

2. Preheat grill for high heat.

3. Lightly oil grill grate. Place tuna steaks on grill, and discard remaining marinade. Grill for 3 to 6 minutes per side, or to desired doneness.

Grilled Tuna

Submitted by: **Gordon Holland**

Makes: 4 servings

Preparation: 10 minutes

Cooking: 6 minutes

Ready In: 1 hour 16 minutes

"Tuna is available most of the year, so fresh steaks should be easy to come by. Be choosy: a reddish color is acceptable, but flesh with dark spots or streaks should be avoided. As with all great ocean fish, the flesh tends to be dry. Marinate with oil, and avoid overcooking. The timing is critical, as tuna should be served medium rare. Use a kitchen timer."

INGREDIENTS

4 (6 ounce) albacore tuna steaks, 1 inch thick

3 tablespoons extra virgin olive oil

salt and ground black pepper to taste

1 lime, juiced

1/2 cup hickory wood chips, soaked

DIRECTIONS

1. Place tuna steaks and olive oil in a large resealable plastic bag. Seal, and refrigerate for 1 hour.

2. Preheat the grill for medium heat. When coals are very hot, scatter a handful of hickory or mesquite wood chips over them for flavor.

3. Lightly oil grill grate. Season tuna with salt and pepper, and cook on the preheated grill approximately 6 minutes, turning once. Transfer to a serving platter, and drizzle with freshly squeezed lime juice. Serve immediately.

Marinated Tuna Steak

Submitted by: **Carin**

Makes: 4 servings

Preparation: 10 minutes

Cooking: 11 minutes

Ready In: 51 minutes

"This mixture of orange juice, soy sauce, and garlic gives this marinade a wonderful taste."

INGREDIENTS

1/4 cup orange juice

1/4 cup soy sauce

2 tablespoons olive oil

1 tablespoon lemon juice

2 tablespoons chopped fresh parsley

1 clove garlic, minced

1/2 teaspoon chopped fresh oregano

1/2 teaspoon ground black pepper

4 (4 ounce) tuna steaks

DIRECTIONS

1. In a large non-reactive dish, mix together the orange juice, soy sauce, olive oil, lemon juice, parsley, garlic, oregano, and pepper. Place the tuna steaks in the marinade and turn to coat. Cover, and refrigerate for at least 30 minutes.

2. Preheat grill for high heat.

3. Lightly oil grill grate. Cook the tuna steaks for 5 to 6 minutes, then turn and baste with the marinade. Cook for an additional 5 minutes, or to desired doneness. Discard any remaining marinade.

Barbeque Halibut Steaks

Submitted by: **Duane Glende**

Makes: 3 servings

Preparation: 10 minutes

Cooking: 15 minutes

Ready In: 25 minutes

"A simple recipe for barbecued halibut. Soy sauce and brown sugar add a special zip that is uncommonly delicious."

INGREDIENTS

2 tablespoons butter

2 tablespoons brown sugar

2 cloves garlic, minced

1 tablespoon lemon juice

2 teaspoons soy sauce

1/2 teaspoon ground black pepper

1 (1 pound) halibut steak

DIRECTIONS

1. Preheat grill for medium-high heat.

2. Place butter, brown sugar, garlic, lemon juice, soy sauce, and pepper in a small saucepan. Warm over medium heat, stirring occasionally, until sugar is completely dissolved.

3. Lightly oil grill grate. Brush fish with brown sugar sauce, and place on grill. Cook for 5 minutes per side, or until fish can be easily flaked with a fork, basting with sauce. Discard remaining basting sauce.

Grilled Halibut II

Submitted by: **Karen David**

Makes: 6 servings

Preparation: 10 minutes

Cooking: 10 minutes

Ready In: 2 hours 20 minutes

"Halibut fillets marinated in lime juice and herbs are simple and delicious, and perfect for any occasion. Pineapple and mango salsas - or any of your personal favorites - make for a perfect finish fresh off the grill."

INGREDIENTS

6 (6 ounce) fillets halibut

2 tablespoons olive oil

2 tablespoons fresh lime juice

1/2 teaspoon dried thyme

1/2 teaspoon dried basil

1/4 teaspoon dried oregano

1/8 teaspoon dried rosemary

DIRECTIONS

1. Place halibut fillets in a shallow baking dish. In a bowl, whisk together the olive oil, lime juice, thyme, basil, oregano, and rosemary. Pour marinade over fish, cover, and refrigerate 2 to 4 hours.

2. Preheat grill for medium heat. Adjust grate height to between 4 and 6 inches from heat source.

3. Lightly oil grill grate. Remove halibut from dish, and discard marinade. Cook for 5 minutes per side, or until fish can be easily flaked with a fork.

Acapulco Margarita Grouper

Submitted by: **Bill Echols**

Makes: 4 servings

Preparation: 20 minutes

Cooking: 12 minutes

Ready In: 1 hour 2 minutes

"Sea bass or any firm-fleshed fish may be used if grouper is not available. The grilled fish and fresh salsa are terrific when served with grilled corn and margaritas."

INGREDIENTS

4 (6 ounce) grouper fillets

1/3 cup tequila

1/2 cup orange liqueur

3/4 cup fresh lime juice

1 teaspoon salt

3 large cloves garlic, peeled

4 tablespoons olive oil

3 medium tomatoes, diced

1 medium onion, chopped

1 small jalapeno, seeded and minced

4 tablespoons chopped fresh cilantro

1 pinch white sugar

salt to taste

1 tablespoon olive oil

ground black pepper to taste

DIRECTIONS

1. Place fish in a shallow baking dish. In a bowl, stir together the tequila, orange liqueur, lime juice, 1 teaspoon salt, garlic, and olive oil. Pour mixture over fillets, and rub into fish. Cover, and refrigerate for ½ hour, turning the fillets once.

2. Preheat the grill for high heat.

3. In a medium bowl, toss together the tomatoes, onion, jalapeno, cilantro, and sugar. Season to taste with salt. Set salsa aside.

4. Remove fillets from marinade, and pat dry. Brush the fillets with oil, and sprinkle with ground black pepper. In a small saucepan, boil remaining marinade for several minutes. Remove from heat, and strain out garlic cloves. Set aside to cool.

5. Grill fish for 4 minutes per side, or until fish is easily flaked with a fork. Transfer fillets to a serving dish. Transfer the fish to a serving plate. Spoon salsa over the fish, and drizzle with the cooked marinade to serve.

Grilled Sea Bass

Submitted by: **Stephanie**

Makes: 6 servings

Preparation: 20 minutes

Cooking: 20 minutes

Ready In: 40 minutes

"This is a truly flavorful dish with a lovely plate presentation. My mom and I experimented and made this for lunch. It came out so good I promptly went to the fish market so I could make it for my dinner guests that night. YUMMY!"

INGREDIENTS

1/4 teaspoon garlic powder

1/4 teaspoon onion powder

1/4 teaspoon paprika

lemon pepper to taste

sea salt to taste

2 pounds sea bass

3 tablespoons butter

2 large cloves garlic, chopped

1 tablespoon fresh Italian parsley, chopped

1 1/2 tablespoons extra virgin olive oil

DIRECTIONS

1. Preheat grill for high heat.

2. In a small bowl, stir together the garlic powder, onion powder, paprika, lemon pepper, and sea salt. Sprinkle seasonings onto the fish.

3. In a small saucepan over medium heat, melt the butter with the garlic and parsley. Remove from heat when the butter has melted, and set aside.

4. Lightly oil grill grate. Grill fish for 7 minutes, then turn and drizzle with butter. Continue cooking for 7 minutes, or until easily flaked with a fork. Drizzle with olive oil before serving.

Grilled Swordfish with Rosemary

Makes: 4 servings

Preparation: 10 minutes

Cooking: 10 minutes

Ready In: 1 hour 20 minutes

Submitted by: **Vini**

"A simple white wine marinade makes this grilled swordfish special. Rosemary is used in both the marinade and a lemon and olive oil sauce that is drizzled over the fish when served."

INGREDIENTS

1/2 cup white wine

5 cloves garlic, minced

2 teaspoons chopped fresh rosemary

4 (4 ounce) swordfish steaks

1/4 teaspoon salt

1/4 teaspoon ground black pepper

2 tablespoons lemon juice

1 tablespoon extra virgin olive oil

4 slices lemon, for garnish

DIRECTIONS

1. Stir wine, garlic, and 1 teaspoon rosemary together in an 8 inch square baking dish. Sprinkle fish with salt and pepper. Place in the baking dish, turning to coat. Cover, and refrigerate for at least 1 hour.

2. In a small bowl, stir together the lemon juice, olive oil, and remaining rosemary. Set aside.

3. Preheat grill for medium heat.

4. Transfer fish to a paper towel-lined dish, and discard marinade. Lightly oil grill grate to prevent sticking. Grill fish 10 minutes, turning once, or until fish can be easily flaked with a fork. Remove fish to a serving plate. Spoon lemon sauce over the fish, and top each fillet with a slice of lemon for garnish.

meatless mains

Don't let the carnivores have all the fun!
Vegetables and veggie burgers on the grill take
on the same rich, smoky nuances. Give thick
vegetables like jumbo mushrooms and fat
slabs of eggplant plenty of time and moderate
temperatures to become tender and juicy all
the way through. Meatless patties and bread
dough are delicious but delicate, so brush
them with oil and mind the heat for the most
flavorful and flawless vegetarian fare.

Grilled Portobello Mushrooms

Submitted by: **Michael**

Makes: 4 servings

Preparation: 15 minutes

Cooking: 20 minutes

Ready In: 35 minutes

"A good dish that goes with almost anything year round. You can double this recipe and serve as a main dish with rice. Enjoy!"

INGREDIENTS

1/2 cup finely chopped red bell pepper

1 clove garlic, minced

1/4 cup olive oil

1/4 teaspoon onion powder

1 teaspoon salt

1/2 teaspoon ground black pepper

4 portobello mushroom caps

DIRECTIONS

1. Preheat grill for medium heat.

2. In a large bowl, mix the red bell pepper, garlic, oil, onion powder, salt, and ground black pepper. Spread mixture over gill side of the mushroom caps.

3. Lightly oil the grill grate. Place mushrooms over indirect heat, cover, and cook for 15 to 20 minutes.

Grilled Portobello and Mozzarella

Submitted by: **Valerie Kasper**

Makes: 4 servings

Preparation: 15 minutes

Cooking: 25 minutes

Ready In: 55 minutes

"Absolutely simple and delicious as an appetizer or main course! Portobello mushrooms with red sauce, roasted red peppers, and mozzarella cheese make this dish just to die for! Yummm!"

INGREDIENTS

4 portobello mushroom caps

1/2 (8 ounce) bottle Italian salad dressing

1 (14 ounce) jar marinara sauce

1 (7 ounce) jar roasted red bell peppers, drained and sliced

8 slices mozzarella cheese

1/2 teaspoon dried oregano

1/2 teaspoon dried basil

DIRECTIONS

1. Place the mushrooms in a large resealable plastic bag with the salad dressing. Seal, and marinate for at least 15 minutes.

2. Preheat grill for medium-high heat. Heat the marinara sauce in a saucepan over medium heat, and keep warm.

3. Oil the grill grate. Place the mushrooms on the grill, and cook for 7 to 10 minutes on each side, until lightly toasted.

4. Preheat the oven broiler. Spread the bottom of a shallow baking dish or oven-proof plate with just enough marinara sauce to cover the bottom. Place mushrooms in the dish bottom side up, and top with the peppers and remaining marinara sauce. Place 2 slices of cheese on each mushroom, and sprinkle with oregano and basil.

5. Broil for 3 to 5 minutes, or until the cheese is melted. Serve hot.

Portobello Mushroom Burgers

Submitted by: **Bob Cody**

Makes: 4 servings

Preparation: 15 minutes

Cooking: 20 minutes

Ready In: 35 minutes

"The steak of veggie burgers. Serve on a bun with lettuce, tomato, and aioli sauce. Oh yeah!"

INGREDIENTS

4 portobello mushroom caps

1/4 cup balsamic vinegar

2 tablespoons olive oil

1 teaspoon dried basil

1 teaspoon dried oregano

1 tablespoon minced garlic

salt and pepper to taste

4 (1 ounce) slices provolone cheese

DIRECTIONS

1. Place the mushroom caps, smooth side up, in a shallow dish. In a small bowl, whisk together vinegar, oil, basil, oregano, garlic, salt, and pepper. Pour over the mushrooms. Let stand at room temperature for 15 minutes or so, turning twice.

2. Preheat grill for medium-high heat.

3. Brush grate with oil. Place mushrooms on the grill, reserving marinade for basting. Grill for 5 to 8 minutes on each side, or until tender. Brush with marinade frequently. Top with cheese during the last 2 minutes of grilling.

Veggie Burgers

Submitted by: **Jen Parmer**

Makes: 8 servings

Preparation: 15 minutes

Cooking: 20 minutes

Ready In: 1 hour 35 minutes

"Burgers that taste like hamburgers, but without meat! You can replace the Cheddar cheese with Monterey Jack or any other cheese you like. If you prefer, you may use a 1.4 ounce packet of brown broth in place of the soy sauce."

INGREDIENTS

2 teaspoons olive oil

1 small onion, grated

2 cloves crushed garlic

2 carrots, shredded

1 small summer squash, shredded

1 small zucchini, shredded

1$1/2$ cups rolled oats

$1/4$ cup shredded Cheddar cheese

1 egg, beaten

1 tablespoon soy sauce

1$1/2$ cups all-purpose flour

DIRECTIONS

1. Heat the olive oil in a skillet over low heat, and cook the onion and garlic for about 5 minutes, until tender. Mix in the carrots, squash, and zucchini. Continue to cook and stir for 2 minutes. Remove pan from heat, and mix in oats, cheese, and egg. Stir in soy sauce, transfer the mixture to a bowl, and refrigerate 1 hour.

2. Preheat the grill for high heat.

3. Place the flour on a large plate. Form the vegetable mixture into eight 3 inch round patties. Drop each patty into the flour, lightly coating both sides.

4. Oil the grill grate, and grill patties 5 minutes on each side, or until heated through and nicely browned.

Carrot Rice Nut Burger

Submitted by: **Janice Joyner**

Makes: 20 servings

Preparation: 1 hour

Cooking: 1 hour 30 minutes

Ready In: 2 hours 30 minutes

"This is a wonderful alternative to hamburgers. Use organic ingredients! There is a difference."

INGREDIENTS

3 cups uncooked brown rice

6 cups water

1 cup toasted cashews

1 pound toasted unsalted sunflower seeds

1 sweet onion, chopped

6 carrots, chopped

1 tablespoon extra virgin olive oil

salt to taste

DIRECTIONS

1. In a large pot, bring the rice and water to a boil. Reduce heat to low, cover, and simmer 45 minutes.

2. Preheat the grill for high heat.

3. Using a food processor, grind the toasted cashews and sunflower seeds to a fine meal. Transfer to a large bowl. Pulse the onion and carrots in the food processor until finely shredded, and mix with the ground nuts. Place the cooked rice and olive oil in the food processor, and pulse until smooth. Mix into the bowl. Season with salt. Form the mixture into patties.

4. Oil the grill grate. Grill the patties 6 to 8 minutes on each side, until nicely browned.

Nutburgers

Submitted by: **Michael**

Makes: 6 servings

Preparation: 20 minutes

Cooking: 10 minutes

Ready In: 4 hours 30 minutes

"This recipe is a savory vehicle for condiments on a bun. Nutburgers can be grilled, baked, or pan-fried."

INGREDIENTS

3/4 cup water

1 cup bulgur

1/8 cup soy sauce

3/4 cup cashew nuts

3/4 cup unsalted sunflower seeds

1 1/8 cups eggs

1 teaspoon chili powder

2 cloves garlic, minced

1 dash hot pepper sauce

DIRECTIONS

1. In a saucepan, bring the water, bulgur, and soy sauce to a boil. Remove from heat, cover, and set aside for 10 minutes, or until all the liquid has been absorbed.

2. Grind cashews and sunflower seeds in a food processor to a fine meal.

3. In a large bowl, mix the cooked bulgur, ground cashews and sunflower seeds, eggs, chili powder, garlic, and hot pepper sauce. Cover, and refrigerate for 4 hours to blend flavors.

4. Prepare the grill for medium heat.

5. Form the bulgur mixture into 6 patties. To prevent the patties from crumbling, spray a piece of foil with cooking spray, and place on the grill. Grill the patties 10 minutes, turning once, or until heated through and browned. Cooking time may vary according to thickness of patties and heat level.

California Grilled Veggie Sandwich

Makes: 4 servings

Preparation: 30 minutes

Cooking: 20 minutes

Ready In: 50 minutes

Submitted by: **Heather Johnson**

"I came up with this recipe to entertain friends. Since I am a semi-vegetarian and love to BBQ, I am always inventing something new. The first time I made this, my meat-lover friends raved about this dish! I prefer mesquite coals over gas barbeques...however, either works fine."

INGREDIENTS

1/4 cup mayonnaise

3 cloves garlic, minced

1 tablespoon lemon juice

1/8 cup olive oil

1 cup sliced red bell peppers

1 small zucchini, sliced

1 red onion, sliced

1 small yellow squash, sliced

2 (4-x6-inch) focaccia bread pieces, split horizontally

1/2 cup crumbled feta cheese

DIRECTIONS

1. In a bowl, mix the mayonnaise, minced garlic, and lemon juice. Set aside in the refrigerator.

2. Preheat the grill for high heat.

3. Brush vegetables with olive oil on each side. Brush grate with oil. Place bell peppers and zucchini closest to the middle of the grill, and set onion and squash pieces around them. Cook for about 3 minutes, turn, and cook for another 3 minutes. The peppers may take a bit longer. Remove from grill, and set aside.

4. Spread some of the mayonnaise mixture on the cut sides of the bread, and sprinkle each one with feta cheese. Place on the grill cheese side up, and cover with lid for 2 to 3 minutes. This will warm the bread, and slightly melt the cheese. Watch carefully so the bottoms don't burn. Remove from grill, and layer the with vegetables. Enjoy as open-faced grilled sandwiches.

Grilled Poblano Pepper and Mango Quesadillas

Submitted by: **Brenda Thompson**

Makes: 8 servings

Preparation: 15 minutes

Cooking: 40 minutes

Ready In: 55 minutes

"We developed this recipe after trying a similar appetizer at a restaurant in Austin, TX. Depending on the peppers, these quesadillas can be mild and fruity or spicy hot."

INGREDIENTS

16 (10 inch) flour tortillas

1 (8 ounce) package cream cheese, softened

1 mango, peeled and diced

1 fresh poblano pepper, seeded and minced

1/4 cup butter, melted

DIRECTIONS

1. Preheat grill for medium heat.

2. Spread half of the tortillas with about 2 tablespoons cream cheese each. Sprinkle mango and poblano peppers over cheese, and press another tortilla on top. Brush butter over the outside of each quesadilla, top and bottom.

3. Grill quesadillas 5 minutes each side, or until golden brown. Remove from grill, and slice into wedges. Serve warm.

Pita Pizza

Submitted by: **Mindy Pretner**

Makes: 1 serving

Preparation: 5 minutes

Cooking: 15 minutes

Ready In: 20 minutes

"Pita Pizza is a quick snack or meal that can be customized to your liking!"

INGREDIENTS

1 pita bread round

1 teaspoon olive oil

3 tablespoons pizza sauce

1/2 cup shredded mozzarella cheese

1/4 cup sliced crimini mushrooms

1/8 teaspoon garlic salt

DIRECTIONS

1. Preheat grill for medium-high heat.

2. Spread one side of the pita with olive oil and pizza sauce. Top with cheese and mushrooms, and season with garlic salt.

3. Lightly oil grill grate. Place pita pizza on grill, cover, and cook until cheese completely melts, about 5 minutes.

Pizza On The Grill I

Submitted by: **Doug**

Makes: 16 servings

Preparation: 45 minutes

Cooking: 15 minutes

Ready In: 3 hours

"Even with a baking stone, a conventional oven is no match for a professional oven when it comes to making pizza. At home, or rather in your backyard, the grill is the way to go. The heat of a hot grill is perfect, and makes it possible to make incredible pizza at home. Use your favorite toppings, but keep in mind not to overload the pizza. Keep it light. Try it - everything is better on the grill!"

INGREDIENTS

1 (.25 ounce) package active dry yeast

1 cup warm water

1 pinch white sugar

2 teaspoons kosher salt

1 tablespoon olive oil

3 1/3 cups all-purpose flour

2 cloves garlic, minced

1 tablespoon chopped fresh basil

1/2 cup olive oil

1 teaspoon minced garlic

1/4 cup tomato sauce

1 cup chopped tomatoes

1/4 cup sliced black olives

1/4 cup roasted red peppers

2 cups shredded mozzarella cheese

4 tablespoons chopped fresh basil

DIRECTIONS

1. In a bowl, dissolve yeast in warm water, and mix in sugar. Proof for ten minutes, or until frothy. Mix in the salt, olive oil, and flour until dough pulls away from the sides of the bowl. Turn onto a lightly floured surface. Knead until smooth, about 8 minutes. Place dough in a well oiled bowl, and cover with a damp cloth. Set aside to rise until doubled, about 1 hour. Punch down, and knead in garlic and basil. Set aside to rise for 1 more hour, or until doubled again.

2. Preheat grill for high heat. Heat olive oil with garlic for 30 seconds in the microwave. Set aside. Punch down dough, and divide in half. Form each half into an oblong shape 3/8 to 1/2 inch thick.

3. Brush grill grate with garlic flavored olive oil. Carefully place one piece of dough on hot grill. The dough will begin to puff almost immediately. When the bottom crust has lightly browned, turn the dough over using two spatulas. Working quickly, brush oil over crust, and then brush with 2 tablespoons tomato sauce. Arrange 1/2 cup chopped tomatoes, 1/8 cup sliced black olives, and 1/8 cup roasted red peppers over crust. Sprinkle with 1 cup cheese and 2 tablespoons basil. Close the lid, and cook until the cheese melts. Remove from grill, and set aside to cool for a few minutes while you prepare the second pizza.

Thai Charred Eggplant with Tofu

Makes: 4 servings

Preparation: 15 minutes

Cooking: 30 minutes

Ready In: 45 minutes

Submitted by: **Angela**

"This is a very authentic Thai flavored recipe using some European techniques in the preparation, which just makes this recipe a 10 out of 10. It's super delicious!!!"

INGREDIENTS

5 small eggplants

3 fresh green chile peppers

4 cloves garlic cloves, peeled

1 tablespoon chopped fresh cilantro

1 small onion, quartered

3 teaspoons light brown sugar

2 tablespoons lime juice

1 tablespoon vegetable oil

8 ounces tofu, diced

1/2 cup chopped fresh basil

DIRECTIONS

1. Preheat the grill for high heat.

2. Oil the grill grate, and cook the eggplants on all sides until charred and black, about 15 minutes. Remove from heat, and place on a rack to cool. Peel, slice diagonally, and set aside.

3. In a food processor or blender, combine the chile peppers, garlic, cilantro, onion, sugar, and lime juice. Process until smooth.

4. Heat oil in a large skillet over high heat, and add the chile mixture. Reduce heat to medium, and cook for 1 minute. Gently stir in the tofu, ¼ cup of basil, and the eggplant. Cook until heated through. Remove to a serving dish, and garnish with the remaining basil.

side dishes

Main dishes aren't the only thing that should feel right at home on the grill. Move that meat over and make room for side dishes! No need to do the mad dash between kitchen and back yard when you're preparing your whole meal right there over the flames. Packets of potatoes, sweet, smoldering vegetables, and heavenly grilled bread are outstanding ways to round out your cookout.

Marinated Veggies

Submitted by: **Mathilda Sprey**

Makes: 8 servings

Preparation: 15 minutes

Cooking: 15 minutes

Ready In: 1 hour

"A healthy way to grill veggies! Makes a great sandwich too!"

INGREDIENTS

1/2 cup thickly sliced zucchini

1/2 cup sliced red bell pepper

1/2 cup sliced yellow bell pepper

1/2 cup sliced yellow squash

1/2 cup sliced red onion

16 large fresh button mushrooms

16 cherry tomatoes

1/2 cup olive oil

1/2 cup soy sauce

1/2 cup lemon juice

1/2 clove garlic, crushed

DIRECTIONS

1. Place the zucchini, red bell pepper, yellow bell pepper, squash, red onion, mushrooms, and tomatoes in a large bowl.

2. In a small bowl, mix together olive oil, soy sauce, lemon juice, and garlic. Pour over the vegetables. Cover bowl, and marinate in the refrigerator for 30 minutes.

3. Preheat grill for medium heat.

4. Lightly oil grate. Remove vegetables from marinade, and place on preheated grill. Cook for 12 to 15 minutes, or until tender.

Foil Wrapped Veggies

Submitted by: **Marni Rachmiel**

Makes: 10 servings

Preparation: 15 minutes

Cooking: 30 minutes

Ready In: 45 minutes

"Really yummy mixed fall veggies grilled in a foil packet. You'll want to use multiple packets to keep them all to a manageable size. Open the finished packets carefully - the veggies are HOT! Enjoy!"

INGREDIENTS

2½ pounds new potatoes, thinly sliced

1 large sweet potato, thinly sliced

2 Vidalia onions, sliced ¼ inch thick

½ pound fresh green beans, cut into 1 inch pieces

1 sprig fresh rosemary

1 sprig fresh thyme

2 tablespoons olive oil

salt and pepper to taste

¼ cup olive oil

DIRECTIONS

1. Preheat grill for high heat.

2. In a large bowl, combine the new potatoes, sweet potato, Vidalia onions, green beans, rosemary, and thyme. Stir in 2 tablespoons olive oil, salt, and pepper to coat.

3. Using 2 to 3 layers of foil, create desired number of foil packets. Brush inside surfaces of packets liberally with remaining olive oil. Distribute vegetable mixture evenly among the packets. Seal tightly.

4. Place packets on the preheated grill. Cook 30 minutes, turning once, or until potatoes are tender.

Grilled Asparagus

Submitted by: **Larry Lampert**

Makes: 4 servings

Preparation: 15 minutes

Cooking: 3 minutes

Ready In: 18 minutes

"The special thing about this recipe is that it's so simple. Fresh asparagus with a little oil, salt, and pepper is cooked quickly over high heat on the grill. Enjoy the natural flavor of your veggies."

INGREDIENTS

1 pound fresh asparagus spears, trimmed

1 tablespoon olive oil

salt and pepper to taste

DIRECTIONS

1. Preheat grill for high heat.

2. Lightly coat the asparagus spears with olive oil. Season with salt and pepper to taste.

3. Grill over high heat for 2 to 3 minutes, or to desired tenderness.

Grilled Tequila Portobello

Submitted by: **Miss BeHavin's Haven**

Makes: 2 servings

Preparation: 5 minutes

Cooking: 10 minutes

Ready In: 45 minutes

"Succulent moist portobello mushrooms do a fiesta of flavor dances sure to enhance any entree."

INGREDIENTS

1/4 cup tequila

1/8 cup unsalted butter, melted

2 tablespoons roasted garlic oil

1 lime, juiced

3 cloves garlic, minced

1 large portobello mushroom, cut into 3/4 inch slices

DIRECTIONS

1. In a small bowl, mix together tequila, melted butter, roasted garlic oil, lime juice, and minced garlic. Let stand for at least 15 minutes.

2. Preheat grill for medium heat.

3. Brush grate with vegetable oil. Brush mushroom slices with tequila mixture, and place on grill. Cook until the mushroom slices begin to wilt, then turn and brush with more of the tequila mixture. Cook for a few minutes, until mushrooms are tender. Watch carefully so they do not burn.

Deb's Spicy Summer Evening Mushrooms

Submitted by: **Deb McQueen**

Makes: 8 servings

Preparation: 5 minutes

Cooking: 10 minutes

Ready In: 1 hour 15 minutes

"This recipe came to be one summer night at a poolside cookout back in southern California. I have been asked for this recipe so many times, I decided to give it to the world. It is tangy, tasty, and even non mushroom eaters have devoured this dish each time I have made it."

INGREDIENTS

2 cups soy sauce

1 cup red wine vinegar

1/4 teaspoon ground black pepper

3 drops hot pepper sauce

2 pounds whole fresh mushrooms

DIRECTIONS

1. In a medium bowl, mix soy sauce, red wine vinegar, ground black pepper and hot pepper sauce. Poke holes in the mushrooms using a fork, then place them in the soy sauce mixture. Cover and marinate in the refrigerator at least 1 hour.

2. Preheat grill for high heat.

3. Lightly oil the grill grate. Place mushrooms on the grill and cook until browned and tender, about 10 minutes.

Grilled Asparagus with Roasted Garlic Toast and Balsamic Vinaigrette

Submitted by: **DJ Williams**

Makes: 4 servings
Preparation: 15 minutes
Cooking: 1 hour
Ready In: 1 hour 15 minutes

"This recipe is delicious during the spring. Even asparagus haters love this one. They do!"

INGREDIENTS

1 medium head garlic, unpeeled

5 tablespoons extra virgin olive oil, divided

salt and pepper to taste

2 tablespoons minced shallot

1¹/₂ teaspoons balsamic vinegar

¹/₂ teaspoon red wine vinegar

1¹/₂ pounds thick stemmed asparagus

4 slices sourdough bread

DIRECTIONS

1. Preheat oven to 350°F (175°C).

2. Coat the head of garlic with 1 tablespoon olive oil, salt, and pepper. Place on a baking sheet, and roast 45 minutes in the preheated oven, until golden brown. Once the garlic is roasted, cut the head in half horizontally, exposing all the cloves. Squeeze both halves into a bowl, discarding any skin. Whisk in 2 tablespoons of olive oil, salt, and pepper. Set aside.

3. While the garlic is roasting, place the minced shallot in a bowl with the balsamic and red wine vinegars for about 30 minutes to let the flavors blend. Whisk in remaining olive oil, and season with salt and pepper. Place asparagus spears in the mixture until ready to grill.

4. Preheat grill for medium-high heat.

5. Place asparagus in a large skillet or directly on the grill. Grill the asparagus, turning over once, until tender, about 10 minutes. While asparagus is grilling, spread the roasted garlic mixture on the bread. Grill bread until toasted. Arrange the bread and asparagus on a plate, and drizzle with the remaining shallot and vinegar mixture.

Tasty BBQ Corn on the Cob

Submitted by: **Deann**

Makes: 6 servings

Preparation: 15 minutes

Cooking: 30 minutes

Ready In: 45 minutes

"This is corn on the cob cooked on the grill with spices and butter. It makes for a yummy side dish to any meal! Try it with fresh garlic and onion."

INGREDIENTS

1 teaspoon chili powder

1/8 teaspoon dried oregano

1 pinch onion powder

cayenne pepper to taste

garlic powder to taste

salt and pepper to taste

1/2 cup butter, softened

6 ears corn, husked and cleaned

DIRECTIONS

1. Preheat grill for medium-high heat.

2. In a medium bowl, mix together the chili powder, oregano, onion powder, cayenne pepper, garlic powder, salt, and pepper. Blend in the softened butter. Apply this mixture to each ear of corn, and place each ear onto a piece of aluminum foil big enough to wrap the corn. Wrap like a burrito, and twist the ends to close.

3. Place wrapped corn on the preheated grill, and cook 20 to 30 minutes, until tender when poked with a fork. Turn corn occasionally during cooking.

Miss Bettie's Zesty Grilled Corn

Makes: 6 servings

Preparation: 20 minutes

Cooking: 20 minutes

Ready In: 40 minutes

Submitted by: **Teresa Johnson**

"This is my mom's recipe for grilled corn. It is tangy and spicy, and the BEST corn recipe I have ever tasted!"

INGREDIENTS

1/3 cup butter

2 tablespoons prepared mustard

1 teaspoon Worcestershire sauce

1/4 teaspoon lemon pepper

2 teaspoons prepared horseradish

6 ears fresh corn

DIRECTIONS

1. Preheat grill for medium heat.

2. In a small saucepan, melt butter or margarine. Stir in mustard, horseradish, Worcestershire sauce, and lemon pepper seasoning.

3. Place each ear of corn on a 13x12 inch piece of heavy duty aluminum foil. Drizzle with butter mixture. Wrap loosely, leaving space for the expansion of steam, and seal.

4. Grill over medium coals for 15 to 20 minutes, or until corn is tender. Small ears will take less time, and larger ears may take more. Carefully unwrap foil, and serve.

BBQ Corn

Submitted by: **Doug Kacsir**

Makes: 10 servings

Preparation: 10 minutes

Cooking: 2 hours

Ready In: 10 hours 10 minutes

"Work that smoker magic on corn on the cob. Be sure to get the corn before the produce person trims off some of the outer husks. The corn must be completely covered by the husk. Use peeled back husks for handles when eating. This recipe multiplies well, and can be used to make corn for a crowd. You will need bagged ice for this recipe to keep the corn cold."

INGREDIENTS

10 ears fresh corn with husks

1 quart beer

1 (7 pound) bag of ice cubes

DIRECTIONS

1. Place whole ears of corn in an ice chest. Pour beer over top. Dump ice out over the ears of corn. Place the lid on the cooler, and let sit 8 hours, or overnight.

2. Preheat smoker to 250°F (120°C).

3. Place corn in the smoker and close the lid. Cook for 1 to 2 hours, turning every 20 minutes or so. Kernels should give easily under pressure when done. To eat, just peel back the husks and use them for a handle.

Southwestern Roasted Corn Salad

Submitted by: **Kim Fusich**

Makes: 8 servings

Preparation: 30 minutes

Cooking: 30 minutes

Ready In: 1 hour 15 minutes

"Corn has never tasted so good! This is a perfect side dish for a BBQ and tastes great on a hot summer day."

INGREDIENTS

8 ears fresh corn in husks

1 red bell pepper, diced

1 green bell pepper, diced

1 red onion, chopped

1 cup chopped fresh cilantro

1/2 cup olive oil

4 cloves garlic, peeled and minced

3 limes, juiced

1 teaspoon white sugar

salt and pepper to taste

1 tablespoon hot sauce

DIRECTIONS

1. Place the corn in a large pot with enough water to cover, and soak at least 15 minutes.

2. Preheat grill for high heat. Remove silks from corn, but leave the husks.

3. Place corn on the preheated grill. Cook, turning occasionally, 20 minutes, or until tender. Remove from heat, cool slightly, and discard husks.

4. Cut the corn kernels from the cob, and place in a medium bowl. Mix in the red bell pepper, green bell pepper, and red onion.

5. In a blender or food processor, mix the cilantro, olive oil, garlic, lime juice, sugar, salt, pepper, and hot sauce. Blend until smooth, and stir into the corn salad.

Grilled Romaine Salad

Submitted by: **Jennifer Glotz**

Makes: 4 servings

Preparation: 30 minutes

Cooking: 2 hours 40 minutes

Ready In: 3 hours 10 minutes

"Romaine hearts are slightly charred on the grill, and served with a fabulous shallot-balsamic dressing. Accompanied with oven dried tomatoes. Whoever eats this will go nuts for it!!!"

INGREDIENTS

1/2 cup olive oil

3 tablespoons white sugar

1 teaspoon dried rosemary

1 teaspoon dried thyme

1/4 teaspoon salt

1/4 teaspoon ground black pepper

8 roma (plum) tomatoes, halved lengthwise

2 shallots, halved lengthwise and peeled

1/2 cup balsamic vinegar

2 tablespoons brown sugar

13/4 cups olive oil

4 romaine hearts

1 tablespoon olive oil

salt and pepper to taste

DIRECTIONS

1. Preheat oven to 225°F (110°C). Mix olive oil, white sugar, rosemary, thyme, salt, and pepper in a large resealable plastic bag. Place tomatoes in the bag, seal, and shake to coat. Arrange coated tomato halves cut side up on a baking sheet. Bake tomatoes 2½ hours in the preheated oven. Remove from heat, and let cool.

2. In a blender or food processor, finely chop the shallots. Add vinegar and brown sugar, and process until smooth. Slowly add 1¾ cups oil, processing frequently, so as to thicken the mixture.

3. Preheat grill for high heat. Brush romaine hearts with 1 tablespoon olive oil, and season with salt and pepper.

4. Place romaine hearts on the preheated grill. Cook 5 to 10 minutes, turning frequently, until slightly charred but not heated all the way through. Serve warm on salad plates surrounded by tomato pieces and drizzled with the shallot dressing.

Cabbage on the Grill

Submitted by: **Debbie**

Makes: 8 servings

Preparation: 15 minutes

Cooking: 40 minutes

Ready In: 55 minutes

"This is a quick way to cook cabbage on the grill. It gets really sweet when cooked this way."

INGREDIENTS

1 large head cabbage

1 1/2 teaspoons garlic powder, or to taste

salt and pepper to taste

DIRECTIONS

1. Preheat grill for medium heat.

2. Cut the cabbage into 8 wedges, and remove the core. Place all the wedges on a piece of aluminum foil large enough to wrap the cabbage. Season to taste with garlic powder, salt, and pepper. Seal cabbage in the foil.

3. Grill for 30 to 40 minutes on the preheated grill, until tender.

Grilled Zucchini and Squash

Submitted by: **Jay Peaslee**

Makes: 3 servings

Preparation: 15 minutes

Cooking: 20 minutes

Ready In: 35 minutes

"Squash and zucchini wrapped in a foil package on the grill. Great when served with steak."

INGREDIENTS

2 zucchini, halved lengthwise and cut in 1/4 inch slices

1 summer squash, thinly sliced

3/4 cup butter

1 tablespoon salt

2 tablespoons ground black pepper

2 tablespoons garlic powder

DIRECTIONS

1. Preheat grill for medium-high heat.

2. Place the zucchini, and squash on a large sheet of aluminum foil, and dot with butter. Season with salt, pepper, and garlic powder. Seal vegetables in the foil.

3. Place the foil pack on the preheated grill, and cook 20 minutes, until vegetables are tender.

Grilled Onions

Submitted by: **Linda Smith**

Makes: 8 servings

Preparation: 15 minutes

Cooking: 1 hour

Ready In: 1 hour 15 minutes

"If you like onions, you'll love this grilled treat! When I barbeque, I like to try and make the whole meal on the grill. This dish can be prepared as an appetizer or a side dish. Enjoy!"

INGREDIENTS

4 large onions

1/2 cup butter

4 cubes chicken bouillon

DIRECTIONS

1. Preheat grill for medium heat.

2. Peel outer layer off onions. Slice a small section off of one end of each onion, and make a small hole in the center. Fill the center of each onion with a bouillon cube and 2 tablespoons butter or margarine. Replace the top of the onion, and wrap in aluminum foil.

3. Place onions on grill over indirect heat, and close the lid. Cook for 1 hour, or until tender. Remove the tops, and cut into bite size chunks. Place in a serving dish with all the juices from the foil.

Grilled Potatoes and Onion

Submitted by: **Bob Cody**

Makes: 4 servings

Preparation: 15 minutes

Cooking: 30 minutes

Ready In: 45 minutes

"Always cook up a package of potatoes and onions with the rest of your grilled meal! Start early, because it takes about a half an hour to cook. These cook over indirect heat (off to the side), so you can grill other things at the same time."

INGREDIENTS

4 potatoes, sliced

1 red onion, sliced

1 teaspoon salt

1 teaspoon ground black pepper

4 tablespoons butter

DIRECTIONS

1. Preheat grill for medium heat.

2. For each packet, measure out 2 or 3 squares of aluminum foil large enough to easily wrap the vegetables, and layer one on top of the other. Place some of the potatoes and onion in the center, sprinkle with salt and pepper, and dot with butter. Wrap into a flattened square, and seal the edges. Repeat with remaining potatoes and onion.

3. Place aluminum wrapped package over indirect heat, and cover. Cook for approximately 30 minutes, turning once. Serve hot off the grill.

Grilled Garlic Potatoes

Submitted by: **Kelly Cetnarski**

Makes: 4 servings

Preparation: 15 minutes

Cooking: 25 minutes

Ready In: 40 minutes

"This grilled potato recipe is so moist and delicious. It goes great with any meal or on its own, but my favorite is with steak. The cheese tops it off perfectly. Add mushrooms and carrots for an excellent variation. Delicious with sour cream on the side."

INGREDIENTS

6 medium baking potatoes, peeled and thinly sliced

1 large white onion, sliced

3 tablespoons butter, sliced

3 cloves garlic, minced

1 teaspoon chopped fresh parsley

salt and pepper to taste

1 cup shredded Cheddar cheese

DIRECTIONS

1. Preheat grill for high heat.

2. Arrange potato slices, separated by onion and butter slices, on a large piece of aluminum foil. Top with garlic, and season with parsley, salt, and pepper. Tightly seal potatoes in the foil.

3. Place on the preheated grill, and cook 20 minutes, turning once, or until potatoes are tender.

4. Sprinkle potatoes with Cheddar cheese, reseal foil packets, and continue cooking 5 minutes, until cheese is melted.

Scalloped Potatoes for the BBQ

Submitted by: **Priscilla Sullivan**

Makes: 4 servings

Preparation: 15 minutes

Cooking: 30 minutes

Ready In: 45 minutes

"A simple and quick way to enjoy the family favorite without using the oven. Note: If you wish, you can make 4 individual foil packets, but be careful - these will cook much more quickly!"

INGREDIENTS

4 red potatoes, thinly sliced

1 large onion, chopped

4 cloves garlic, chopped

1/4 cup chopped fresh basil

1/4 cup butter, cubed

salt and pepper to taste

DIRECTIONS

1. Preheat grill for medium heat.

2. Layer sliced potatoes on aluminum foil with the onion, garlic, basil, and butter. Season with salt and pepper. Fold foil around the potatoes to make a packet.

3. Place potato packet on heated grill over indirect heat, and cook for 30 minutes, or until potatoes are tender. Turn over packet halfway through cooking.

Easy Cheesy Potatoes

Submitted by: **Pat**

Makes: 6 servings

Preparation: 15 minutes

Cooking: 30 minutes

Ready In: 50 minutes

"This is a great side dish to any barbecue. Potatoes are grilled with peppers and onions in a foil package. It cooks on the grill along with your favorite barbecued main dish."

INGREDIENTS

6 potatoes, thinly sliced

1 small onion, chopped

1/4 cup chopped green bell pepper

salt and pepper to taste

1/4 cup butter or margarine

1 cup shredded Cheddar cheese

DIRECTIONS

1. Preheat grill for medium-high heat.

2. Coat one side of a piece of aluminum foil large enough to hold all the potatoes and vegetables with cooking spray. Place the potatoes, onion, and green bell pepper in the center of the foil, and season with salt and pepper to taste. Then place small pats of the butter or margarine over the vegetables.

3. Carefully seal all the edges of the foil around the vegetables to form a packet. (Note: Double wrapping will help to prevent burning.)

4. Place packet on the preheated grill, and grill for 20 minutes. Turn packet, and grill for 10 more minutes.

5. Carefully open packet, check for tenderness with a fork. If tender, sprinkle the cheese over the vegetables and allow it to melt. Transfer to a platter, and serve with your main entree.

BBQ Potato Roast

Submitted by: **Christine Dekoning**

Makes: 5 servings

Preparation: 10 minutes

Cooking: 35 minutes

Ready In: 45 minutes

"This is an all time favorite with everyone I have ever served it to. Seasoning and oil may be changed depending on taste preference. Serve with sour cream."

INGREDIENTS

10 potatoes, peeled and halved

1/2 cup vegetable oil

2 tablespoons seasoned salt

DIRECTIONS

1. Preheat grill for high heat.

2. Place potatoes in a large saucepan with enough lightly salted water to cover. Bring to a boil. Cook 15 minutes, or until tender but firm.

3. Drain potatoes, and pat dry. Coat thoroughly with vegetable oil and seasoned salt.

4. Place potatoes on the preheated grill. Cook approximately 20 minutes, turning periodically.

Naan

Submitted by: **Mic**

Makes: 14 servings

Preparation: 30 minutes

Cooking: 7 minutes

Ready In: 3 hours

"This recipe makes the best naan I have tasted outside of an Indian restaurant. I can't make enough of it for my family. I serve it with shish kabobs, but I think they would eat it plain."

INGREDIENTS

1 (.25 ounce) package active dry yeast

1 cup warm water

1/4 cup white sugar

3 tablespoons milk

1 egg, beaten

2 teaspoons salt

4 1/2 cups bread flour

2 teaspoons minced garlic (optional)

1/4 cup butter, melted

DIRECTIONS

1. In a large bowl, dissolve yeast in warm water. Let stand about 10 minutes, until frothy. Stir in sugar, milk, egg, salt, and enough flour to make a soft dough. Knead for 6 to 8 minutes on a lightly floured surface, or until smooth. Place dough in a well oiled bowl, cover with a damp cloth, and set aside to rise. Let it rise 1 hour, until the dough has doubled in volume.

2. Punch down dough, and knead in garlic. Pinch off small handfuls of dough about the size of a golf ball. Roll into balls, and place on a tray. Cover with a towel, and allow to rise until doubled in size, about 30 minutes.

3. During the second rising, preheat grill to high heat.

4. At grill side, roll one ball of dough out into a thin circle. Lightly oil grill. Place dough on grill, and cook for 2 to 3 minutes, or until puffy and lightly browned. Brush uncooked side with butter, and turn over. Brush cooked side with butter, and cook until browned, another 2 to 4 minutes. Remove from grill, and continue the process until all the naan has been prepared.

Unbelievable Grilled Garlic Bread

Makes: 12 servings

Preparation: 15 minutes

Cooking: 20 minutes

Ready In: 35 minutes

Submitted by: **Kimber**

"French bread (or Italian) is lightly toasted, spread with a creamy cheese mixture and grilled until warm, melted, and unbelievably delicious. The finished bread keeps well in an airtight container."

INGREDIENTS

1 cup mayonnaise

6 cloves garlic, peeled and minced

3/4 cup grated Parmesan cheese

1/2 cup shredded Cheddar cheese

1 tablespoon half-and-half

1/4 teaspoon paprika

1 (1 pound) loaf French bread, halved lengthwise

DIRECTIONS

1. Preheat grill for medium heat.

2. In a medium bowl, mix the mayonnaise, garlic, and Parmesan cheese. In a saucepan over medium-low heat, mix the Cheddar cheese, half-and-half, and paprika. Stir constantly until melted and smooth. Pour into the bowl with mayonnaise mixture, stirring until well blended.

3. Place the French bread on the grill cut side down, and let it toast for a few minutes. Remove from the grill, and spread the cheese mixture on each side. Place the halves back together, and wrap the loaf in aluminum foil. Return to the grill for about 15 minutes, turning occasionally, until the loaf is heated through and the cheese mixture is hot.

desserts

Don't douse the flames yet; it's time for a sweet finish to your flame-kissed feast. Fruit's natural moisture and sweetness make it a perfect grill companion: juices gush while sugars turn to toasty caramel and flavors deepen. And when you're in the mood for a little sweet indulgence, get ready for a deluxe twist on classic s'mores. Sweetness and heat go so well together, you'll never want to grill again without saving room for dessert!

Barbequed Pineapple

Submitted by: **Michael Fischer**

Makes: 8 slices

Preparation: 15 minutes

Cooking: 15 minutes

Ready In: 8 hours 30 minutes

"Barbequed Pineapple! Serve in bowl or banana boat with pineapple on either side, and a scoop of ice cream or two with juice glaze on top. You may substitute juice (1/2 cup) for sugar and rum part of marinade."

INGREDIENTS

1 fresh pineapple

1/4 cup rum

1/4 cup brown sugar

1 tablespoon ground cinnamon

1/2 teaspoon ground ginger

1/2 teaspoon ground nutmeg

1/2 teaspoon ground cloves

DIRECTIONS

1. Peel the pineapple and, leaving it whole, cut out the center core. Slice into 8 rings, and place them in a shallow glass dish or resealable plastic bag. In a small bowl, mix together brown sugar, cinnamon, ginger, nutmeg, and cloves. Pour over the pineapple, cover, and refrigerate for 1 hour, or overnight.

2. Preheat grill for high heat.

3. Lightly oil grill grate. Grill pineapple rings 15 minutes, turning once, or until outside is dry and char marked. Serve with remaining marinade.

Grilled Peaches

Submitted by: **Karen**

Makes: 4 servings

Preparation: 20 minutes

Cooking: 18 minutes

Ready In: 38 minutes

"This is a very simple, yet delicious end to a grilled meal. Peaches are grilled with a balsamic glaze, then served up with crumbled blue cheese. A sophisticated, yet extremely simple recipe. Perfect for summer entertaining!"

INGREDIENTS

3 tablespoons white sugar

3/4 cup balsamic vinegar

2 teaspoons freshly ground black peppercorns

2 large fresh peaches with peel, halved and pitted

2 1/2 ounces blue cheese, crumbled

DIRECTIONS

1. In a saucepan over medium heat, stir together the white sugar, balsamic vinegar, and pepper. Simmer until liquid has reduced by one half. It should become slightly thicker. Remove from heat, and set aside.

2. Preheat grill for medium-high heat.

3. Lightly oil the grill grate. Place peaches on the prepared grill, cut side down. Cook for about 5 minutes, or until the flesh is caramelized. Turn peaches over. Brush the top sides with the balsamic glaze, and cook for another 2 to 3 minutes.

4. Transfer the peach halves to individual serving dishes, and drizzle with remaining glaze. Sprinkle with crumbled blue cheese.

Skewered Cantaloupe

Submitted by: **Lol**

Makes: 4 servings

Preparation: 15 minutes

Cooking: 6 minutes

Ready In: 21 minutes

"Don't turn your nose up at this dish. Melon grills beauti-fully, and the minty sauce takes it to the next level. For a great dessert, serve it with big scoops of vanilla ice cream."

INGREDIENTS

1 cantaloupe - peeled, seeded, and cubed

1/4 cup butter

1/2 cup honey

1/3 cup chopped fresh mint leaves

skewers

DIRECTIONS

1. Preheat grill for medium heat.

2. Thread the cantaloupe chunks onto 4 skewers. In a small saucepan, heat butter with honey until melted. Stir in mint. Brush cantaloupe with honey mixture.

3. Lightly oil grate. Grill skewers 4 to 6 minutes, turning to brown all sides. Serve with remaining sauce.

Figs Oozing with Goat Cheese

Submitted by: **Linda**

Makes: 4 servings

Preparation: 15 minutes

Cooking: 3 minutes

Ready In: 18 minutes

"Fresh figs stuffed with succulent goat cheese, wrapped in grape leaves, roasted on the grill, and drizzled with honey. For an extra oomph of flavor, skewer the figs on rosemary fronds. One bite and you'll feel as if you've reached nirvana!"

INGREDIENTS

8 fresh figs

1/2 cup goat cheese, softened

8 grape leaves, drained and rinsed

1/2 cup honey

skewers

DIRECTIONS

1. Preheat grill for medium heat.

2. Make a small incision in the bottom of each fig (large enough to hold pastry bag tip). Place goat cheese in pastry bag with plain tip. Fill figs with goat cheese by squeezing a small amount of cheese into the bottom of each fig. The figs will plump up when filled. Wrap each fig with a grape leaf, and skewer 2 to 3 figs on each skewer.

3. Lightly oil the grill grate. Place fig skewers on hot grill. Cook for 2 to 3 minutes, turning once. Drizzle with honey, and serve.

Bellyful of Barbecued Bananas

Submitted by: **Charlie**

Makes: 4 servings

Preparation: 15 minutes

Cooking: 6 minutes

Ready In: 21 minutes

"Throw some of those bananas on the barbi! A scrumptious dessert that will make your tastebuds jump for joy! Try pouring a drop of your favorite liquor over the bananas and ice cream just before serving."

INGREDIENTS

4 bananas

1 tablespoon lemon juice

1 cup brown sugar

1 teaspoon ground cinnamon

2 cups vanilla ice cream

DIRECTIONS

1. Preheat grill for low heat.

2. Halve each of the bananas lengthwise, then widthwise. Sprinkle bananas with lemon juice. In a small bowl, mix together the brown sugar and cinnamon. Roll banana pieces in sugar/cinnamon mixture until well coated.

3. Lightly oil the grill grate. Arrange bananas on preheated grill, and cook for 3 minutes per side. Serve in a bowl with vanilla ice cream topped with a sprinkling of remaining cinnamon/sugar mixture. Yum!

Campfire Banana Splits

Submitted by: **Toni Blyth**

Makes: 6 servings

Preparation: 10 minutes

Cooking: 8 minutes

Ready In: 18 minutes

"This was a recipe from my old Girl Scouting days. A very easy recipe for all ages that needs little adult supervision. Great for sleep-overs and backyard camping trips."

INGREDIENTS

6 large bananas, unpeeled, stems removed

2 cups semisweet chocolate chips

1 (10.5 ounce) package miniature marshmallows

DIRECTIONS

1. Preheat the grill for high heat.

2. Spray 4 sheets of aluminum foil, large enough to wrap bananas, with cooking spray.

3. Slice the peel of the banana from stem to bottom, while slicing the banana inside lengthwise. The bananas can be cut into slices instead if you like (while still in the peel) for easier handling later.

4. Carefully open the banana just wide enough to place the chocolate chips and marshmallows inside the peel with the banana. Stuff with as much of the chocolate chips and marshmallows as desired.

5. Wrap the bananas with the aluminum foil and place on the grill or directly in the coals of a fire. Leave in long enough to melt the chips and the marshmallows, about 5 minutes. Unwrap bananas, open the peels wide, and eat with a spoon.

Rich S'mores

Submitted by: **Lucy**

Makes: 4 servings

Preparation: 10 minutes

Cooking: 5 minutes

Ready In: 17 minutes

"Take the classic s'more to a new level! Homemade oatmeal cookies, rich chocolate and marshmallows. The campground classic will never be the same."

INGREDIENTS

8 large oatmeal cookies

4 ounces milk chocolate

8 large marshmallows

skewers

DIRECTIONS

1. Preheat grill for high heat.

2. Place 1 ounce of chocolate on the flat side of 4 of the oatmeal cookies. Skewer the marshmallows, and roast them, turning constantly, until they are a golden brown all over.

3. Slide a warm marshmallow onto the chocolate and top it with another cookie (flat side down). Repeat for all cookies. Let sit for a couple of minutes to melt chocolate, and serve.

recipe contributors

index

credits

the staff at allrecipes

Jennifer Anderson
Barbara Antonio
Mary Ashenden
Justin Bross
Emily Brune
Tess Bruney
Scotty Carreiro
Sydny Carter
Jill Charing
Jeff Cummings
Julie Dey
Kirk Dickinson
Tim Hunt
Nathan Kaiser
Richard Kozel
Jim Kreyenhagen
Kala Kushnick

Judy Mahtaban
Elana Miller
Carrie Mills
Bill Moore
Yann Oehl
Lesley Peterson
David Plesha
Alicia Power
Stephanie Schrader
Maya Smith
Carl Trautmann
Scott Walter
Esmee Williams
Krista Winjum
Sarah Young
A. K. Zebdi

thanks

The staff would like to thank David and Hillary Quinn, whose comments and feedback have made this a better book.

the allrecipes tried & true series

Our *Tried & True* cookbooks feature the very best recipes from the world's greatest home cooks! Allrecipes.com, the #1 recipe website, brings you the "Best of the Best" dishes and treats, selected from over 24,000 recipes! We hand-picked only recipes that have been awarded 5-star ratings time and time again, so you know every dish is a winner.

Current titles include:

Allrecipes Tried & True Favorites; Top 300 Recipes

Filled with the best-loved recipes from Allrecipes.com - these have all won repeated standing ovations from millions of home cooks and their families, intrepid eaters and picky kids alike.

Allrecipes Tried & True Cookies; Top 200 Recipes

Enjoy the world's best cookie recipes and invaluable baking tips and tricks that will turn anyone into an expert on preparing, decorating and sharing cookies. With over 230 cookie recipes, you'll find tried and true recipes for all your old favorites, and lots of new favorites too!

Allrecipes Tried & True - Quick & Easy; Top 200 Recipes

Great-tasting meals in minutes! This cookbook features delicious dishes that can be prepared in minutes. Discover the joys of cooking without spending hours in the kitchen!

Allrecipes Tried & True - Thanksgiving & Christmas; Top 200 Recipes

So many treasured holiday memories are made around the table! For Thanksgiving dinners, family breakfasts, Christmas parties and more, rely on this collection of beloved favorites that have stood the test of time.

Allrecipes Tried & True - Slow Cooker & Casserole; Top 200 Recipes

Within the pages of this cookbook you'll find recipes for exceptional casseroles and slow cooker that offer the best in both convenience and crowd-pleasing flavors, just right for weeknight dinners, potlucks and family gatherings.

Allrecipes *Tried & True* cookbooks are available at select bookstores, by visiting our website at http://www.allrecipes.com, or by calling 206-292-3990 ext. #239. Watch for more *Tried & True* cookbooks to come!

Allrecipes.com · 400 Mercer, Suite 302 · Seattle, WA 98109 USA · Phone: (206) 292-3990